The Opinionated Gardener

CAMPANULA NITIDA, *dwarf form of* C. PERSICIFOLIA.

The Opinionated Gardener

RANDOM OFFSHOOTS FROM AN

ALPINE GARDEN

GEOFFREY B. CHARLESWORTH

with drawings by

LAURA LOUISE FOSTER

DAVID R. GODINE
Publisher · Boston

First edition published in 1988 by
DAVID R. GODINE, PUBLISHER, INC.
Horticultural Hall
300 Massachusetts Avenue
Boston, Massachusetts 02115

The drawing of *Silene hookeri* on p. 125
is used courtesy of Hunt Institute for
Botanical Documentation, Carnegie-Mellon
University, Pittsburgh, Pennsylvania, and
Timber Press, Inc., Portland, Oregon.

Library of Congress Cataloging in Publication Data
Charlesworth, Geoffrey.
The opinionated gardener.
1. Alpine gardens. 2. Rock gardens. 3. Alpine
gardens—Massachusetts. 4. Rock gardens—Massachusetts.
I. Title.
SB459.C42 1988 635.9'672 86-46253
ISBN 0-87923-672-8

FIRST EDITION
Printed in the United States of America

Contents

❧ I I I ❧
The Philosophy of the Garden

❧ I V ❧
Mixed Seeds

CONTENTS

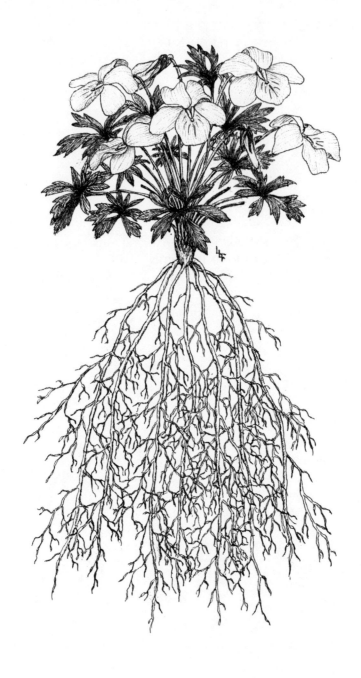

VIOLA PEDATA VAR. LINEARILOBA *(concolor)*,
deeply cut leaves.

Preface

I HAVE BEEN helped as a gardener by many writers and friends. Such help usually takes the form of an opinion; no gardener is very dogmatic. Our interests are varied and intense, our tastes are well considered but tolerant and likely to evolve throughout our gardening lives. Our methods, if successful, are designed for our own gardens, climates, and ways of life. The title of the book attempts to emphasize this point of view. If my experiences and prejudices are helpful or inspiring to the reader, I shall be more than satisfied, but writing a recipe for success has not been one of my aims. Gardeners are very kind to each other's efforts and will admire in somebody else's garden things they would not admit in their own. If any of these essays are pointedly critical, it is of some aspect of gardening I would not or could not do myself, or of some fashionable attitude that is unexamined.

My own garden is 1,400 feet above sea level in southwestern Massachusetts. The spot is in hardiness Zone 5, with temperatures dropping occasionally to −20 degrees Fahrenheit, and often to −10, although seldom for long stretches of time. Snow is plentiful but not reliable. The seasons are well marked with anomalies such as a thaw in January or occasional frosts in early June or late August. Although we get well over 40 inches of rain annually, there can be a drought at any time of year. The soil is a rather poor acid sand that drains well.

I share my garden with Norman Singer, at one time the national secretary of the American Rock Garden Society, and with numerous wild animals. The garden is surrounded by forest, and animals are the most destructive force in the garden throughout the year.

Other people mentioned in the text are members of the American Rock Garden Society. I would like to thank them and all the other gardening friends, in particular Buffy Parker, who have encouraged me to write these essays, and of course Norman Singer, without whose hard work and unselfish enthusiasm this book would not exist. Thanks too, to Laura Louise (Timmy) Foster for allowing use of her previously unpublished drawings.

This collection of essays began as contributions to the newsletter of the Connecticut Chapter of the American Rock Garden
Society. The emphasis is therefore on growing alpine plants.
My English background may explain any idiosyncratic language
in the text.   G.B.C.

ANEMONELLA THALICTROIDES, *Rue Anemone, has white and
pink forms and double forms of both colors.*

❦ I ❧

The Seasons of the Garden

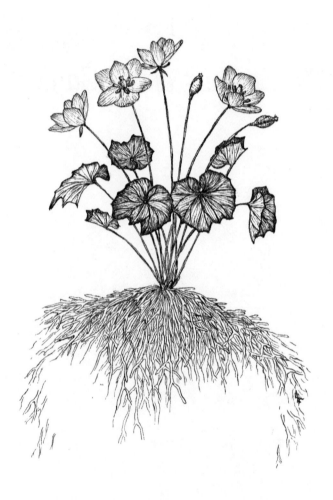

JEFFERSONIA DUBIA, *one of the earliest flowers to bloom that doesn't come from a bulb. This east-Asian plant is a soft lilac color.*

Home Thoughts from Abroad

WHEN WE READ Browning's famous words: "O, to be in England / Now that April's there," gardeners empathize instantly. What a ghastly time to be away from the garden. Our feelings cool a little as we go on to read that his concern is for "the brushwood sheaf round the elm-tree bole" and not at all for the *Jeffersonia dubia* and the drabas now burgeoning in the rock garden. By the time we reach the second stanza and realize that the poet is also missing May, it becomes clear that Browning has badly mismanaged his life or at least his vacation and is going to spend the two most important months of the year in Italy instead of attending to the transplanting and weeding that would be the normal activity for those of us caring for even a basic garden.

These pangs of anxiety and depression are common enough even in January, when home thoughts from abroad emanate from Florida beaches or wherever you have gone to escape the blasts of a New England winter. Will the snow cover stay? Shouldn't I be home shoveling snow onto the raised beds? And the cold frames! Will the lids stay on? Did the pots go into the winter wet enough? What if there is a thaw? Will the plants warm up enough to start growing, and shouldn't there be a thicker cover of boughs over each one? One of the worst anxieties of all is over what will happen to the seedlings that started sprouting in October and November. The books are always harping on the sow-the-seed-fresh theme, and it is true that some seed seems to sprout more vigorously in October than if left until March. But whatever does one do with the pots once the seeds have germinated? Two possibilities are to grow them on under lights or to try a sunny window. This second method is madness if you aim to have seeds sprouting in October. The seedlings would be certain to stretch and wilt before transplanting time, and you would have a bunch of invalids not worth the trouble of calling a doctor.

Sowing under lights is a good method if you are there to water every day and if you can and will spray for aphids. One great device is to have a fan blowing over the pots twenty-four hours a day. You can transplant the seedlings when they are quite small, too, for you are already committed to maximal care.

But none of this works at all if you go to Florida or the islands for two weeks. People talk about neighbors and nieces who come in every day to water, but we all know that not even another rock gardener would give your babies the attention they need and deserve, so there is always an element of lottery involved in any trip south, no matter how brief. My solution is to do everything I can before I leave and then turn my psychological back on my plants. But Browning obviously knew what was what. I can't seem to forget, not really forget.

I had some good things coming along in November and December. They were in three-inch pots sunk into sand in cold frames. The lids of the frames are rather sketchy by now. Originally they were made of Lucite, an expensive, rigid, fully transparent plastic. For one season the lids were perfect, but by the time the wind had blown them around a few times and a few small objects had dropped on them, cracks and then breaks appeared. By now the lids are a motley of Lucite remnants, plastic bags stapled on the frames, chicken wire to represent rigidity, Ross netting to keep out leaves, and rocks and logs to hold them down. The hinges went long ago. The horizontal winter wind and inquisitive snowflakes go under the lids without let or hindrance. What will happen to those seedlings? I sanguinely expect some will survive and some will perish. At this point I start to rationalize: I don't really want plants whose seedlings are tender, so it doesn't really matter whether they die or live. But of course that isn't true. I know I shall chide myself for not holding back the sowing of the tenders until February or March, or at the very least saving half the seeds and sowing them twice.

And what about the garden itself? Will the meager branches I left on the beds catch and hold the snow? Maybe I should have collected fresh evergreens instead of using last year's naked boughs. But that would have required a full week's work at a time when the leaves had to be shredded and the cold frames filled, the woodpile replenished, the barn cleaned, and the wood chips laid down for the paths.

But at least I might have taken extra pains for a few specials? Not even! Everything I did had number-one priority all the way through mid-December; there wasn't time to cut even one branch. I did manage to wrap up a couple of dwarf conifers in burlap. These are two which normally come out of the winter looking like lepers: *Chamaecyparis "Boulevard"* and *Juniperis communis Compressa Nana*. The winter burn is always an eyesore. The little Noah's Ark tree juniper usually greens up again by early summer, but the blue chamaecyparis takes much longer. This is the first time I have ever bound them, and they look like the feet of some unhappy Chinese princess. I hope a similar distortion doesn't result from this cosmetic protection.

Does one really want these demanding aristocrats? I think the juniper is such an angel, the only conifer that stays really dwarf for a dozen years at least, with character to match its stature. It is as engaging as a toy poodle. Many gardens have it, but it never grows stale. It never overwhelms anything, even your best androsaces. The chamaecyparis is expendable. It has already been warned that if it grows much more or continues to need more attention than it deserves, it will have to go. The associated problems are: chop or dig? If dig, who will? when? and where to? My ploy for getting it dug and removed in November was fine on paper, but nothing actually took place. A root-pruning encirclement of the tree is a prerequisite for a successful transplant job. This was not done, so any attempt at removal in the spring will be a hack-and-pull job, like a surgeon with a bread knife.

The weather forecast has just been on television. Did you realize that forecasters in Florida gloat over wintry events in Minnesota and Massachusetts? Snowbirds watch these forecasts gleefully. I feel a different sort of glow as I imagine inches and inches of protective snow accumulating on the raised beds, protecting my plants from harsh winds and temperature changes, and hiding from view all the half-finished weeding, the botched jobs. Saying once and for all you can't do anything more until spring!

So, Browning, I think you ought to get back there and get busy. Quit all this messing about in Florence and Pisa, or wherever you are. Those suckers on the elm tree need pruning. If you wait until the whitethroat and the swallows return, you are going to face a jungle. And don't you think you are being a bit patronizing about the local flora—"this gaudy melonflower," indeed!

If Browning were a real gardener I could share his disassociation from the exotic local gardens. If I visit a garden in Seattle I get a strong urge to rush back to my own garden and do something. But in Florida I feel I am looking at a garden landscape I could never emulate and have no need to envy. The bougainvillea and the odd azalea do not stir me. The only quiver comes from seeing a yellow composite roadside weed—is it a rudbeckia? Could I grow it? Shall I look for seed?

The big pull north from Florida is the prospect of all the seedlists and catalogs accumulating in my mailbox. I have nightmares that all the good stuff will have been snapped up before my order gets processed. Some days the feeling is so intense I think of getting in the car and driving non-stop to Sandisfield post office to check the arrivals. I have a fantasy of writing my orders right there and heading south again. If you are a gardener you can always find an excellent reason not to travel. If any of your friends and loved ones has a fear of travel there is an excellent solution to the problem. Encourage rock gardening! Then all fear and guilt, all explanations and justifications that beset these phobic souls would be dissipated forever. Enthusiasm for this new-found hobby would rule out trips to Florida and eliminate all anxious thoughts about what is happening in the real world under the snows of New England. On second thought maybe I should develop a travel phobia of my own.

January: De Profundis

WITH THE FIRST substantial snowfall comes a change in the personality of the gardener. There is the garden with its strange contours, unplanned, unanticipated, mysterious, inviting us to emerge and admire. If we succumb to the beauty and try to get close to it, we destroy it with footprints. Worse, we hear the snapping of labels underfoot, for the footpaths are obliterated, and we forget the local geography. Five or six years ago I ran over one of my cold frames, breaking pots and a plastic cover. Joie de vivre dwindled, and self-recrimination followed. If your ground is still unfrozen you can protect vulnerable spots with those reflecting lollipops. If you are too late and the ground is hard, a large plant pot filled with sand will hold a reflector and act as a warning.

In addition to the "don't-spoil-it-all" reason for keeping out of the garden there is the general discomfort of plodding through drifts and the inhospitality of January weather. Nevertheless I have enjoyed garden visits in the depths of winter. Roxie Gevjan's well-known Philadelphia garden is a wonderland of dwarf conifers which manage to look even more poetic in snow than in the growing season. Winter is a good time to take stock of your evergreens and decide which must be moved and whether the presence of another would be effective. Most of our garden interaction in winter is with the part of it which sticks up above the snow and is visible from the house. It is worth thinking about. If your garden is big enough you can have fun touring on snowshoes or cross-country skis.

But as I started to say, the gardener's personality changes: we lose interest in a situation we cannot change and want to postpone thinking about solutions until they can be put into effect. January compensates by being the month of seedlists and catalogs. The action called for is rereading notes taken in the spring and summer, researching names, reading books and journals, planning new beds and revisions of established beds. In other words, constructive dreaming. For me, the climax of the month is a winter-study weekend organized by the American Rock Garden Society. The snows of January are temporarily forgotten, and a surge of anticipation for the new season takes over.

Ahead of spring is February, the month of light, when the combination of leafless trees, snowy ground, longer days, and a sun circling higher and higher in the sky fools us into thinking light means heat. At this time an alpine house becomes a promised land of shoots and buds; you can believe in flowers when they're under glass, and you know the cycle of life is poised to start afresh. An alpine house makes the same demands on us as a dog or a child. You leave it reluctantly and always with extreme anxiety, and if somebody else agrees to take care of it, the anxiety increases. The rewards too are mixed: one is either intensely happy, as when a rare bulb blooms, or spectacularly miserable fighting aphids with spray cans. When the unexpected happens and *Anchusa caespitosa* blooms you can force no one into coming over to look at it as the roads are icy and a nor'easter is predicted. Like gardening only more so. I quote from two of our alpine-house enthusiasts.

Ed Leimseider: "By all means get an alpine house, it will change your life." True.

Eloise Lesan: "Yes, the tropaeolum bloomed, but nobody could get up my hill to look at it." Tough.

Fat in February

WHAT DO GARDENERS do in winter? They accumulate fat. The last real, backbreaking, exhausting exercise most of us do in the fall is raking up the leaves and stuffing them into plastic bags. This entails an enormous overuse of the stomach muscles, aggravated by the plastic's refusal to stay either vertical or open. Energy is expended in raising each leaf to bag-mouth height at least once, and packing down has to be done at frequent intervals. There are other more energy-efficient ways to gather leaves. Some use an internal-combustion engine, but engine noise on a limpid fall afternoon destroys all pleasure for oneself and for every neighbor within half a mile in all directions. More to the point, it is the "work" one does in the garden that is the pleasure. "Work" equals physical work. We used to sing a hymn at school: "Who sweeps a room as for thy laws makes that and the action fine." Whatever one's attitude to "work," the October and November cleanup is the last chance to keep fit without the humiliation of aerobic exercises. The Thanksgiving opener to the orgies of winter is the beginning of the end of Fitness. We doubtless need a layer of winter fat as much as chipmunks do, but it is usually in place long before the gross excesses of late December.

By January one's only major movement is the daily walk to the mailbox to send off the seed orders. Most evenings are spent slumped in a chair reading reference books and catalogs and sorting slides, with occasional time out to watch young urban athletes doing their aerobic exercises on television. I long to join them in their jolly, ridiculous kickings and flailings, but the floor of this oldish house is not too sound, and no catastrophe is more unnerving than introducing workmen into the house in winter to do repairs. If the snowfall is a reasonable depth, if the surface has the right texture, if the sun is shining and the wind is calm, one can spend a half-hour putting on cross-country skis and another half-hour cross-country skiing across the garden. More time spent at this activity would be excessive, as the odds in favor of an ungraceful accident increase rapidly with time. Skiing takes place about three times a winter. The rest of the winter is a waiting period for March. The breaks in this time span are for Rock Garden meetings. There everyone talks about plants, complains about the food, and eats compulsively. The food has been paid for, the company is intoxicating, the holiday syndrome is present in every detail. By March all doubt about serious overweight has vanished.

As the snow and ice melt and dissolve with the first warm days and nights and the first rain showers, we make forays into the inhospitable garden looking for ways to burn off the calories. Unfortunately nearly everything you do in March is an error. Too soon you rake off the leaves from the beds. The fresh green mats you uncover will brown and wither within the month. You take off protective boughs, hotcaps, and burlap with dire consequences. You clip back the winterkilled ends of the heathers—and by May the whole plant could be dead. You rake up leaves from the lawn, leaving indelible footprints in the muddy ground and compressing the soil. You take down the snowfence and invite the deer to enjoy an unseasonably early freedom of access to the fresh green salad of your favorite iberis. The cold frames are opened to the first rain and the warm sun. But do you really want those young plants to break dormancy? There will surely be another snowstorm, there will surely be record-breaking low temperatures and gale-force winds before April ends. Even raising the cold-frame lid for a quick peek will disturb the lid sufficiently to allow the next gale to blow it off, and there will be a sickening squeak as the Lucite breaks. You unearth the containers from their makeshift winter shelter to check for visible life and urge them on. They will hate your concern two weeks later when the temperature drops to 5 degrees.

But the lure of activity is irresistible. The minor disasters seem a small price to pay for the right to garden. This season is also the turning point for the weight curve. March and April will see a leveling off and then the start of a slow descent to the slim normalcy of August. See your doctor in August; if you can't get a good checkup then, it is useless to try in February while you are still winter's fool.

February Madness and Tool Buying

TOWARDS THE END of February, and well before the last major snowstorm, we have an irresistible urge to get into the garden. A brief thaw sends us rushing around the yard, poking through dead leaves and snow remnants to search for shoots of bulbs or anything else that might be stirring. It is a hopeless scene; there is nothing to do except inwardly bubble and fume. Some relief is obtained by a visit to a garden center. No nursery will have anything living for sale until late March. I remember when I lived on Long Island driving many miles at the end of March to Martin Viette's nursery and feeling very foolish for arriving before the plants. To save face one looks instead at gardening tools, trying to exorcise the demon winter by buying something as an inauguration rite. In this vulnerable and high-strung state of mind I have bought most of the tools I possess. Many are useless, so here follows a rundown of what a gardener need *not* buy and of a few things a beginner will not regret owning. Vegetable gardeners can freely ignore most of what follows.

First on the not-needed list are the big items. Don't buy a ten-horsepower rototiller. They make enough havoc in new ground to fool you into thinking you can grow carrots, but one year of rototilling will only get the ground ready for potatoes. It takes a few years of good management before you have a decent, weed-free bed, and there are better ways of starting a rock garden. Nor will you need those antique-looking push cultivators. I don't ever use a hoe, either—these tools are all for vegetable people. A hand cultivator with three claws, preferably of flexible wire, is perhaps the most useful tool for scratching soil and removing weeds. A weeder is also useful for removing taprooted weeds and all those verbascums and papavers you planted yourself which are now taking over.

The next big item not to buy is a tractor mower. Get rid of the grass. If you want a bit of grass, restrict it to the amount you can cut with a push power mower or, for a quiet, worry-free time, a push non-power mower. The walk is healthier than the ride if your knees can stand it. Do not buy an electric mower, the cord is lethal to flower beds. Other gadgets which look good in the store but don't pay the rent are electric edgers, electric chain saws, electric hedge clippers, and all kinds of spreaders. This is a bit sweeping: the hedge clippers might come in handy. But wouldn't you be better off if you got rid of whatever it is you need them for?

I would not recommend a wheelbarrow. Two-wheel carts can do nearly everything a wheelbarrow can do, and you are not required to be a strong-armed acrobat to maneuver one. On the other hand, a wheelbarrow can negotiate a few places a cart cannot.

For a long time I saw no use for a trowel, although I bought one religiously every February. Now I see they are essential for carefully digging up a plant for a show, or to give it away, or to replant it. A spade would serve the same purpose but doesn't have the finesse of a trowel.

Tools you do need are spades, shovels, and forks. I think a spade with a square end and one with a pointed end are both essential. A shovel is useful but less necessary since one of the spades will substitute. Forks are a bit special too, but sooner or later a digging fork is needed as well as a fork to handle mulch, manure, etc. The latter should have finer tines and a shovel shape. Other occasionally used tools are mattocks, sledgehammers, and crowbars. For some properties these could be invaluable.

Also cutting implements: edge clippers, pruning shears, pruners, grass shears one-handed and two-handed, knives, scissors. I lose a lot of each every year and have to replace rusty scissors left on a stone or clippers and pruners thrown on the compost heap with the trash. You should buy brightly colored hand tools or spray paint them fluorescent, but even if you do, small tools come with a guarantee that they will be left outside five percent of the growing season.

More things you don't need are clothes specially shaped for gardening. On the hanger in the store or in the mail-order catalog those huge pockets and tiny pockets, side pockets, back pockets, shin pockets, thigh pockets, those aprons, bags, and tool carriers look so seductive you wish you had thought of them first and taken out a patent. They all fail you in the end, however. You can't reach tools in the deep pockets, or you find yourself kneeling on a knife. Things in aprons fall onto favorite plants. Crouching and bending, hard enough at the best of times, become exercises in contortion and sometimes in masochism. There are no solutions. You may find a quaint costume you can live in, but don't expect miracles. As for shirts with pockets: has anyone solved the problem of eyeglasses' falling out? Has anyone solved the problem of gradual fill with soil and sticks? Do you remember to remove pencils and labels before tossing your shirts in the laundry? And yet shirts without pockets are unthinkable.

Kneelers are a mixed blessing. Yes, you do need them for planting out in April when the ground is cold and wet. Yes, you will leave them lying around while you wander to another part of the garden, and as you do the wind will casually blow the kneepad on to the androsace bed. You can't get away with substitutes such as newspaper, plastic sheets, burlap, or plywood. They are either absorbent, fragile, painful, or even more destructive than a kneeler. The kneepad kind, which supposedly remain permanently encircling your knees, either have elastic tight enough to cut off the circulation or are so loose they drop to your ankles the minute you rise.

Buy rakes in quantity. You need rakes for making beds and paths. More than one size is useful, as are a bamboo rake for leaves and a wire rake for getting leaves off the beds. Buckets!

I have never counted them, but we have at least forty in use constantly. Plastic buckets are useful, as are washing-up bowls and kitty-litter trays. Equip yourself with baskets and trugs if you are into flower picking.

Don't forget gloves in your February shopping spree. Rubber gloves for making containers, leather gloves if you grow cactus, but plenty of cotton gloves. A thorn under a nail can waste a couple of hours' gardening time. You don't have to weed and dig with gloves on, but you always want to have them available; they transform your hand into a tool.

Well, I don't honestly think any of the above will actually stop impulse buying in February. I love garden centers, I even browse the pesticide section for as long as I can hold my breath. So far I have resisted Chipmunk Crossing signs, but this is another year, and you never know how February madness will strike.

A March Walk

SOME YEARS AGO the snow left the garden before the end of March, but the ground stayed hard and cold, and the spirit raged, impatient for outside activity. The forest which bounds the garden is a tangle of wild raspberry, fallen trunks, alder whips, and chunky ferns. The best time to wander through it is mid-winter when the boggy ground is hard and snow fills the treacherous hollows. Spring is wet, summer buggy, and fall belongs to the hunters. Nobody does much wandering then.

That March we looked at a stretch of the forest just below the cleared land and thought we might convert it into a year-round Ramble, a glade we could amble through at any season with impunity and even with pleasure. So out came the loppers, the pruning saws, the axe and the machete, and we had a week of glorious toil hacking out a path. By "path" I mean a yard-wide swath you could walk through without kicking, stumbling, or stooping. We called it the March Walk. By April the weather warmed up, and we got back to what life is all about—real gardening, not slinging sticks.

We didn't use the March Walk again that year and forgot

about it until the following March. By then Nature had been hard at work replacing the raspberry canes and placing a few more tree corpses across the path. We cleared up a bit, but the writing was on the wall. If you don't use a path you lose it. And you have to use it throughout the year, not just when a guest wants a change from watching you garden.

Five years later there isn't a trace of the March Walk. The memory of it evokes two conflicting emotions. One is a kind of rejoicing over the astounding resilience of Nature. It seems no matter what we do to the forest there is no need for guilt: Nature will do on-the-spot repairs and laugh at our incursions. The sobering corollary, of course, is that while Nature easily recovers from a dose of clearing by mere gardeners, there is no assurance that damage on a larger scale will not be irreversible. Man makes deserts. The other reflection occasioned by the March Walk is the poignant realization that the garden itself will follow the March Walk into oblivion. I am reconciled to this, though; we are here by invitation to enjoy the artifact we call a garden, but the land itself can never be anything but borrowed for a few years.

When we first moved to Massachusetts, I used to go into the woods on tiptoe trying to avoid treading on the erythronium leaves and the trilliums and wondering if each plant was some treasure to be preserved. Now I can make a March Walk and realize it doesn't really matter what I do to modify Nature's disgraceful tangle. She/He will win in the end.

Rain

IS THIS THE worst spring in living memory? We are past the middle of May and still haven't had a good rain all year. After a winter with very little snow there has been less than an inch to wash away snow and winter dirt and get the plants off to a new season. The good part is that the weather has been perfect for gardening: no mud, no wet grass, no carpet of weeds to contend with. The bad part is the state of anxiety as storm after storm misses us and the plants begin to show signs of stress. It happened this way last year too. Is it a new pattern?

Gardeners are constantly complaining about the weather. During our drought last spring gardeners in southern Connecticut were complaining about the excess rain that kept them out of the garden weekend after weekend. This is my sixteenth spring in this garden, and I thought I understood the weather patterns fairly well. Our forty-plus inches of rain could be relied on to obviate all watering except when planting out (provided the garden could survive a couple of droughty periods in July and August). True, a bit of hose work seemed to be needed, especially for the benefit of the gardener, but not much seemed to die because of drought. Now I am beginning to wonder. Our short-term experience of weather—even a lifetime in the same locality—cannot guarantee that the weather we think we know and think we know how to work around will continue year after year. It only needs a mild aberration statistically speaking to foul up our expectations and hopes. People who recall severe winters, wet summers, and droughts, are usually gardeners with something at stake vulnerable to such extremes.

I sometimes think, "What did I do wrong to deserve this drought?" Perhaps I ordered too many plants during January, more than I can take care of. It is certainly true that I cannot take care of the plants I did order. The drought makes watering imperative if the babies are going to come through, but they are scattered far and wide—too far for real care. Nature seems to be out there punishing my confidence by not coming up with the rain I relied on to keep them alive.

My own rain dance consists of: not wearing a jacket when it looks like rain, watering the seed pots on days rain is predicted, and never putting buckets under the eaves of the barn. This is so that the rain gods cannot accuse me of presuming too much. Some nights I leave out my garden cart, hoping that by morning it will be filled with water—a small sacrifice to the rain gods. If I feel specially daring I leave my favorite scissors in the cart.

I never think my neighbor down the road is the one responsible for the drought. But in fact there may be a case of matricide or incest I am unaware of. I may not have sufficient information about their personal lives. But since none of them have had a very extensive garden for at least two years, the drought seems unlikely to have been engineered just to punish them.

Our operative priests are the weather forecasters, especially the television types. During really important weather events I watch three channels in succession to get opinions from the three cities whose signals reach us. I try to read, between the weather maps and the cloud patterns of the satellite pictures, what kind of weather my garden will get. Like most priests, however, ours are imperfect. In a general kind of way their forecasts are correct; but they seem to feel a need to sound definite and believable, so they reduce their predictions to a "most likely" case with the alternatives glossed over or left unsaid. Their interest is quite parochial and is centered on the local city. Just occasionally our garden is included, but it seems to be only an afterthought.

The worst sin these high priests commit is to direct their irritating chatter to golfers, the spectator-sport crowd, parade goers, and marathon runners. They adopt a smarmy demeanor when we are enduring drought and make hysterical apologies whenever there is a "threat" of rain, as though to take partial credit for the weather. This in spite of the occasional unconvincing disavowal that they are *really* responsible. You would think these people didn't know where their drinking water comes from. Because they are trying to please this pleasure-crazed group, their predictions are sometimes vividly colored, and the message to gardeners may be misleading. How often I have delayed watering on the strength of that non-materializing shower threatening to spoil a baseball game or a parade. How often have I failed to cover tender plants because the city boys had it "in the thirties" and didn't tell me I would get 28 degrees. So part of my weather worship consists of dashing to radios at ten past the hour and TV sets at twenty past the hour and trying to forecast from the forecasts what the weather in our garden will really do.

When rain finally comes, the edginess that has been building up fades away to be replaced by a calm, contented, soggy glow. Finally the pressure is off to be hyperactive; finally, there is no decision to make about watering, or anything else for that matter. Nature is taking care of everything. Good old Nature. After it is clear that the rain has really started there are always a few chores to do outside. Put buckets under the eaves of the barn to catch the water. Check to see that plants are not sitting in bowls and trays without drainage. Check to see that nothing is covered that should be exposed to the rain. Collect all the perishable and rustable items left lying around. In the process the first few drops fall like balm on the head, but very soon—in less than five minutes—getting wet becomes unpleasant. The end of outdoor chores is an uncomfortable dash into shelter and dry clothes. The sound of rain outside is a symphony of splashes, trickles, tinkles, gurgles, and drips. Indoors all the plans I made to do cleanup chores as soon as rain started go by the board. I just sit listening. Anyway it is always too dark to clean out a closet or read a book. Better just sit and gloat.

Some people plant out in the rain. Some people weed. I hate the feeling of plastic around my neck and legs. I hate drips from rain hats. I hate wet knees, and most of all I hate getting bitten by a black fly or a mosquito just as my hands are muddy. Black flies crawl into one's ears when one is most defenseless. So I usually leave the rain to the insects, the robins, and the swallows. I like the enforced rest. On fine days I want to be outside, I must be outside. In a drought I get very tired; I need the rain rest. There is an old story about God making the world in six days and resting on the seventh. In my version God worked every day until it rained, then he took a rest. I can't believe God would wait until the weekend to take his first rest; Sunday might have been fine, and it might have rained the following Wednesday. Not being bound by all the conventions humans have to put up with, God must surely have done the sensible thing. Or perhaps it really did rain the first Sunday!

Well, the rain finally came on May 17. Blessed day. I had done a pretty thorough rain dance the evening before: no buckets under the eaves, of course; seed pots thoroughly watered; covers on all the trays to minimize the benefits in case rain fell; plants left out in kitty-litter trays without drainage. But the clincher, I think, was the buckets of stone. I am trying to get the garden covered with a mulch of three-eighths-inch stone. The stone is shoveled into buckets and carted to each bed in turn. A bucket of dry stone is just manageable; wet, it is pretty heavy. That evening I filled the buckets and left them by the beds, so naturally they filled with rain. Nature had to be waiting for that final touch of spite.

Anyway, the rain changed my character. I suddenly felt mellow, healthier, my walk had a slight bounce, and I sat around smiling over little things. At last I would have something to write to my sisters about—the rain! It turned out to be only .6 inch, but the happiness could hardly have been greater for a full inch or more. Yes, I know the amount because there was a rain gauge out. It had been part of an earlier rain dance *not* to put out rain gauges, but I eventually compromised and but out one of them. I can now coast for a week at least. The seed pots have regained their normal weight and lost that feathery Styrofoam feeling. Since the rain, seeds have been sprouting madly, lupins and primulas. Every plant needs both warmth and moisture. I suppose one should just say "of course," but instead it seems more appropriate to brood about the miracle of the plant life cycle and stop thinking about weather as an enemy. Part of the miracle is that some of the seeds have the sense to wait until the soil is moist enough before deciding to break loose.

Meanwhile spring in retrospect has been glorious. The garden has never looked better. Every fruit tree bloomed its head off, including two pears that hadn't bloomed in fifteen years. One wild apple bloomed for the first time we could remember, with flowers all the way up its trunk like plastic flowers on a Mayday float. Forsythia bloomed all the way to the top, and the magnolia had enough in reserve to survive two frosts with a few fat flowers. Just a half inch of rain can change the worst spring in memory into the best ever. What a fickle lot gardeners are.

Spring

"APRIL, APRIL,/LAUGH thy girlish laughter;/Then, the moment after,/Weep thy girlish tears." These lines now hint of sexism and ageism, but the gist of the couplet remains good sense. While the weather is capricious and undependable, the plant kingdom delights us with surprises yet baffles our predictions. Plants have survived that books say couldn't, and there are losses none can explain. Before you accept the evidence before your eyes, be warned: many plants that seem to have survived the winter unscathed die before the end of April. Many plants that seem to be dead in April need time before they show new growth, and it may be May before the first shoot comes through or the grey mat greens. So temper your own laughter and tears with patience and prudence. The sempervivum munched to the nub by animal neighbors will grow back, the buds stripped from the rhododendrons obviously won't flower. Do not poke at the plants you think may be still alive; give them time to revive from dormancy. Don't clip back branches that seem to be winterkilled too soon, it could be the worst "care" you could provide. Shrubby penstemons don't want to be pruned this early, nor does *Daphne cneorum*. Leave raoulias and even phlox to green up in peace with minimal ministrations. Wait for aquilegias, physoplexis, trilliums, and anything that dies down to a resting bud to emerge; try to keep your fingers away from the crowns. I once knew a woman who used to open flower buds to peek at the color, but her touch was far lighter than mine.

By mid-month the big push has started with your seed pots, and there will be many, many seedlings to watch, enjoy, and attend to, especially if you had pots indoors or in a sheltered place. By now nearly all the penstemons, primulas, lewisias, and dianthus will have germinated, but on no account should you discard unsprouted pots. Sporadic germination takes place through the summer, and in any case all unsprouted pots should be kept another winter. Even if you had the misfortune to lose the first flush of seedlings through too much or too little care, it is still possible that further germination may occur; again, keep the pot. When you start serious transplanting towards the end of the month, or more likely in May, you will have to face the difficult problem of how many seedlings to transplant. A rule of thumb for me is to do about fourteen or fifteen, maximum, and leave the rest in the original pot. After fifteen you really get tired of doing the same species if you have others competing for your attention. Do more than you need, however, for there will be losses, and you will have plants to give away. On the other hand it sometimes seems a waste of time to pot up thirty or forty fairly ordinary plants. Devaluation accompanies overproduction. I break this rule with primulas. I don't remember ever throwing away a primula. There is always someone who wants them because we all have a part of the garden where we want a big display, and primulas are often the answer. If the seedlings are of some rather rare plant, always do transplant all of the seedlings; you will have no trouble finding willing foster parents for your babies.

Do you keep a record of what you are doing in the garden? I have kept a jumble of information for the last twenty years in what I loosely refer to as a "journal." Every April there is an entry somewhere mid-month which announces the first "nice day" of the year. I remember the glorious blue days of icy January and the promise of spring the day after a rain in March, but it isn't until this first "nice day" that one can truly repossess the garden after the long absence. You must still be on the lookout for frosts, be ready to open and close the cold-frame lid and the alpine-house windows and doors. It is a good time to sort out the cold frame, but be conservative about discards. Be prepared, too, for putting branches back on the beds if you had such protection over the winter. Welcome back the swallows and the drabas, also welcome the UPS man with the box of plants you forgot you ordered. When plants arrive by mail, plant them in pots and keep them out of the sun for at least a couple of weeks before planting them in the garden. George Schenk, in his book *The Complete Shade Gardener*, recommends using clay pots for this purpose: "imperviable plastic may cause rotting by holding too much moisture around the plant's crown." I find plastic pots don't need as much watering and are cheaper and lighter.

High Season

"NOW IS THE month of Maying when merry lads are playing"; but not rock gardeners. May is the climax of our year, the month of reckoning when we finally take stock of

SANGUINARIA CANADENSIS. *The bloodroot is
an early spring ephemeral.*

successes and failures. Fortunately there is such an abundance in May that we can pass off as a mere trifle the few miscalculations, the occasional misfortune. As we rejoice, we take stock critically and dispassionately of the Grand Scheme of the garden. At last we admit to ourselves that some plants will not return. Why? Was it really a disaster or will life go on without them? Is something wrong fundamentally? Can it be corrected next year? Soil? Exposure? Is it the plants' fault?

May is the climax of the year. All our planning was directed towards what the garden looks like now. Impulsive major changes are out of the question. But many good ideas are born this busy month that must be given time to mature. Gardening is a process even in May, for a garden is never a finished object. Don't forget to look at it. Find time to stand and stare.

The north of our region is about two weeks behind the south at the beginning of the month. By the end of the month the gap has closed somewhat, and by mid-June peonies are blooming throughout Connecticut. In the north in early May, *Phlox subulata* starts, so do arabis, aubrietas, saxifrages, jeffersonia, pulsatilla. The hummingbird returns to feed on *Rhododendron P.J.M.*, and *Trillium erectum* and *Erythronium americanum* grace the woodland roadside. By the end of May the first garter snake makes its appearance, and you can watch the chipmunk eating your crocus bulbs as they ripen. The grand parade of primulas that started with *P. denticulata* and the Julianas in early April continues with the Candelabras as May ends.

May has two horrors. One is mowing the grass. The ideal garden has no lawns at all; but it is a brave suburbanite who has the courage to dispense with lawn entirely, and if you garden in a field as I do, grass is simply unavoidable, so mowing is the only alternative to encroaching woodland, and, worse than woodland, hardhack. Unfortunately, mowing has such a powerful cosmetic effect that one goes on doing it. City gardeners should be sensible enough to eradicate all lawn. If you really have to sit, or worse sunbathe, plan a small square of wood chips or concrete.

The other horror is the black fly. The two defenses, insect repellent and bee hats, are nearly as bad.

JEFFERSONIA DIPHYLLA *blooms a little later than* J. DUBIA.
The flowers are very fleeting.

In May think about next May. Start collecting seed for the seed exchange; *Eranthis hyemalis* will be ready by month-end, and from then on there is something ripening every week. Start cuttings. Try all kinds of methods. Use a mixture of coarse sand with a little peat or Jiffymix, or use pure sand or perlite. Try using flats, pots, boxes, or the open ground. Try covering with plastic, or make a "crystal garden" with jam jars inverted over the cuttings. If you can work in a greenhouse use a mister or mist by hand with an atomizer. The idea is to keep the atmosphere moist until roots form; therefore, no direct sunlight if you can avoid it. Try planting parts of varying length from quite short half-inch tips to a six-inch chunk or a whole rosette. The submerged part should have the leaves removed to prevent rot, but saxifrages and heathers don't seem to mind if they are left on. There are a lot of books that give you confidence, but the best strategy is to try a few methods. You usually won't have a lot of cutting material, and you don't need a lot of successes—just one or two make you feel good. Many books are aimed at nurserymen with money to buy sophisticated apparatus who want more than a plausible ritual to turn misters and meristems into gold. Propagation by seed, cuttings, or division is the next step after making a garden, and in its own way gives as much pleasure. Your gardening friends will appreciate your efforts at propagation when you give them your extras.

Chipmunks or woodchucks will sometimes burrow under a mat-forming plant in the middle of a bed. A deterrent which may work is a piece of rag soaked in the dirty oil from a lawn mower or cultivator. Stuff it down the hole and cover with a stone. Woodchucks can be quite persistent, so you need patience. Watch for mole runs. Every year nearly every rhododendron has a mole run circling it, especially if the mulch is fairly heavy. Disturbed plants don't suffer too much while the spring moisture is in the ground, but if you fail to see the tunnel or ignore it you will lose plants. Runs don't seem to be permanent, and when the soil is pushed in again it will usually stay put. One year I struggled with a determined mole for two weeks before it abandoned one particular highway. One partial solution to the chipmunk problem is to plant bulbs you particularly want examples of in twos and threes in several places. You don't get a drift effect, but you may get to keep a few bulbs next year.

Weeding is at a high point in May. Don't treat weeding as a demeaning chore as vegetable people and border people do. Weeding gives you the opportunity to get close to the plants. As you do it, renovate the labels and plant out all those new plants that came by mail or from your own seedlings. In fact you can indulge the possessive passion of the collector by taking a census. You will cut down drastically on weeding if you mulch. Use an appropriate mulch, that is, coarse sand or small stone for the alpines, and organic material such as cocoa hulls or shredded leaves for woodlanders and primulas. Mulch encourages worms, which delight moles, which make runs for mice; there is always a tradeoff.

CLAYTONIA VIRGINICA. *The Spring Beauty is widespread in eastern North America.*

Early Summer

IN JUNE WE breathe a sigh of relief. The rock garden is "finished." The imperatives of planting out, weeding, preparing for shows are behind us. Well, there is a *little* bit of truth in that; the rhododendron freaks are still elated, but the choicest rock plants are fading, forming seed, and growing into relaxed mops rather than the tight buns that emerged from winter. Are we to imagine that they are loosening up to allow the stale lowland air to circulate better, deprived as they are of the stiff gales of the mountain tops? The growth is real, though, in the sense that plants get bigger. The aristocrats of the rock garden, the androsaces, drabas, douglasias, and so on will grow but not always noticeably. On the other hand, alyssums, phlox, aubrietas, campanulas will often expand to double their April length and breadth. You must watch that these hearty beauties don't overrun defenseless buns. These border disputes need constant attention. Once the flowers fade, you tend to forget the significance of green boundaries and can lose *Androsace mathildae* under an advancing *Asperula pontica*. I suppose that ideally one should place every plant with exactly the amount of room it will need as a mature specimen, but the vicissitudes of mortality make this aspiration futile. Besides, we want the ground well covered *now*, not three years from now. So we end up planting "too close." Cut back the vigorous spreaders; many of the crucifers benefit by the trimming. You also get cutting material—more than you want, sometimes. If a plant roots down as it sprawls, get a few rooted cuttings too, but keep them in sand until the roots are well formed.

Of course the idea of the garden being finished by Memorial Day is absurd. For one thing the campanulas are just beginning; the dianthus are peaking, and this is the month of penstemons and Asiatic primulas. Other plants to grow for June bloom are codonopsis, phyteuma, meconopsis, eremurus, allium, aethionema, silene, late phlox, and many others. What I am getting at is that even if you are a diehard perennial-border lover and imagine June to be synonymous with peony, iris, poppy, lily, and daylily, you might remember some of the rock-garden competition. The glare of color emanating from the border may be more competition than the gentler alpines can take, so it is

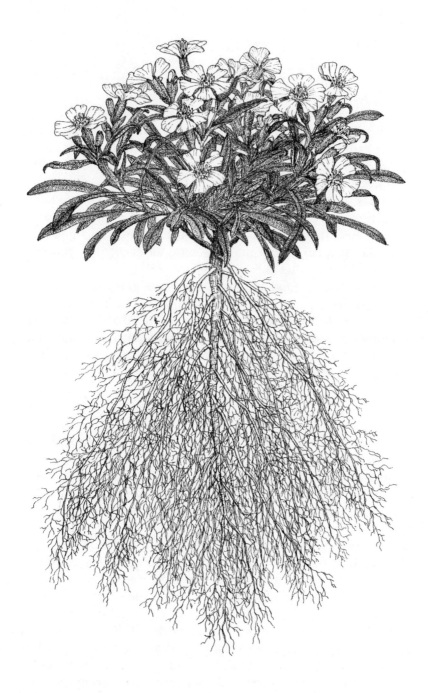

SILENE CAROLINIANA SSP. WHERRYI, *a beauty from the eastern United States for a dryish position in sun or shade.*

a good idea to keep the rock garden some distance (visually? psychologically?) from the perennial border.

By July you may be wishing you had a few annuals to carry on the display. Get to know the annuals other people grow and beg a little seed for next year. A few good ones to look for are dyssodia, eucharidium, *Crepis rubra*, gilia, *Delphinium tatsienense*, and a good number of mimulus species. If you find petunias, marigolds, and zinnias irresistible when you go to the local nursery, put them in the perennial border or in a separate cutting bed; they don't look right with alpines, and a good, fat petunia can easily kill a precious bun, an event that you may not notice until after the first frost.

June is also a good time to show your garden and to visit other people's gardens. Call ahead of time; don't show up unexpectedly. Most gardeners like to appear civilized when guests are present even if they affect a Garden of Eden costume when no one else is around. Take a gift, naturally, but also take a tray or a box, and plastic bags, just in case.

End of Summer

DID YOU SPEND August loafing? We got just enough rain to keep the weeds coming. On the whole that is better than a dry-as-dust drought. I have been planting out without hindrance from the weather. Animals are another story; today the entire planting I labored over yesterday was dug up and strewn hither and yon.

There is always a question about when one should plant out. My guidelines are: 1.) moist ground or rain predicted; 2.) good-sized plants; 3.) temperature under 82 degrees. Tiny seedlings will not establish in high summer, but if the roots are coming out of the pot bottom and screaming to be planted, the plant would probably be happier in the garden. Once the roots fill the pot, drying out is very rapid, and you have to water just about every day it doesn't rain. The alternative would be to pot on into a larger pot, but that always seems a major undertaking to be reserved for plants you plan to overwinter in a frame. If you keep a pot in full sun the danger is increased, but on the

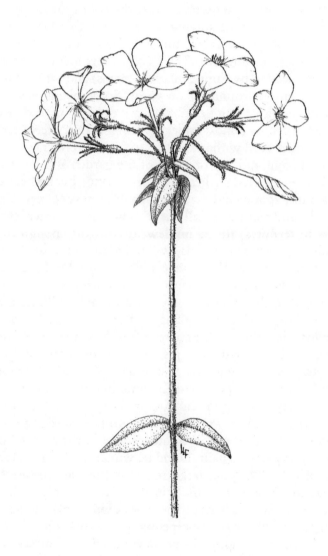

PHLOX STOLONIFERA, *for open woodland, in muted pinks and blues.*

other hand plants in deep shade get leggy, and slugs are lurking in shadier spots. A lath house is one compromise. You could also lay a length of snowfence over the cold frame.

It is a bit late to be solving the problem for this year. You have either got your babies through the summer or you blew it. Slugs can eat quickly. They have a short menu of preferred delicacies headed by campanula, oxytropis, and astragalus. The best penstemons round off the meal. Some plants never seem affected, though I don't doubt slugs would even tackle cactus.

Weeds are now almost under control—that is, I feel I can stop and pull one weed without having to face an acre. This is partly because I have mulches on most of the garden and most of the paths. These include a heavy layer of sand, buckwheat hulls, cocoa hulls, spoiled hay, wood chips. Neatness counts. Visitors have gloomily criticized all these mulches: not thick enough, brings in termites, forms mildew, cakes hard enough to keep the rain out, brings in weeds, will only last a year. Well, it may all be true, but mulches solve problems for a brief period, and I will face the dire consequences as they arise.

The end of the planting season is a variable. Ultimately you have to decide whether a plant is safer in the garden or in an alternative location such as a cold frame or an alpine house. I have seen shrubs that were just stuck under a tree and totally neglected survive a winter and summer unharmed. The iris you discarded on a compost heap blooms like magic, but the one you lovingly planted in late August heaves and rots. Perhaps the trickiest genus is *Primula*. Many primula seedlings and divisions will have been planted out already by the end of August; probably any that remain should be wintered in the cold frame. Even plants with quite large root systems can be heaved by frost at any time during the winter. April is an especially dangerous time. Small plants can be held down by placing flat rocks around their crowns. Some people put a rock directly on the primula crown, although I have never tried that. Success would depend on removing the rock at the right time. The primula problem is so acute that you may want to plant out only year-old speciments. I prefer to have plants bloom in the garden even if it means losing a few.

Fall

As October begins, Nature's most remarkable metamorphosis act is unfolding in the airspace above the garden. No floral relics of the first frosts can compete with the sumptuous display of the trees. The whisper becomes increasingly noisy as the first crisp leaves gently release their hold and flutter down. One day near mid-month there will be a strong north wind, and suddenly the sky will be blue and the ground gold. The new light changes every aspect of the garden. The effect is as total as the departure of the snow. The garden moves towards dormancy, and we have the same mixture of sadness and relief as when a well-loved guest leaves. We tidy up, reflect on the pleasure of the encounter, look forward to another reunion, but most of all we enjoy the termination of responsibility.

I usually erect a rampart of snowfence around vulnerable beds while the ground is still soft. The deer are slightly discouraged and seem less likely to invade, especially if evergreen branches are also put in place. The common wisdom advises putting the boughs on after the ground is hard, but I have had no real catastrophe doing this ahead of the freeze. The real purpose of the snowfence is to slow the flakes as they are driven by the wind and have them drop onto a favored bed. The catch is that a snowstorm can come from any direction, even south, and there is no certainty that the snow will accumulate where it is needed. If the strategy works we get deep drifts which often stay the winter through. In April a lot of time is spent kicking stubborn snow patches and repenting too much foresight. Like so much gardening mystique, it makes the gardener feel better for having done something rather than nothing. Whether the deer or winter will cooperate is almost irrelevant.

Snowfence and covered beds give the garden a restful but slightly eery feeling, like a graveyard. The number of ways of getting from A to B is sharply reduced, and soon it becomes impossible to remember the true layout of the garden and exactly where the plants are. This heightens the sense of conclusion to outdoor activities. Whether this is good or bad depends on your temperament. I am happy it is all over.

October is still a work month on good days. After the leaves have flared and fallen there is sweeping and shredding, and it is a good time for edging and weeding. Everything you can do in October is a bonus in April. The earth is still warm (warmish), and a new bed is a pleasure to prepare. It's too late to plant the new bed now, but the bed will be ready to receive the plants you will order to excess in January.

Fred Watson, who gardens in New Hampshire, covers some of his beds with walk-in cold frames. Under these frames he overwinters many choice alpines including New Zealand raoulias and celmisias. Last year I did something similar on a small scale by placing a light aluminum frame over a small section of one raised bed. The plants with this overhead protection were in good shape in the spring. I piled boughs over this minimal plastic protection and made no attempt to keep out cold air. My friend in New Hampshire had a much tighter setup, and winter sun often raised the interior temperature to over 90 degrees. The plants were not subjected to sudden temperature changes and survived the winter well.

There is a whole world of gardening methods waiting to be explored. The concept of winter hardiness needs redefinition. We could drop most current generalizations in favor of descriptive success stories. And then, if ever we learned to bring plants through the winter, we might tackle the more difficult task of getting them through the summer. The alpine-house set have shown us what can be done with plants in pots and benches in the winter and somewhat less successfully in the summer, using artificial heating and cooling devices. How about more experimentation in the open garden?

More plants should be tried outside in New England. Last winter the following came through a Massachusetts winter: *Raoulia glabra, R. lutescens, Kniphofia natalensis, K. galpinii, Brachycome rigidula, Nierembergia repens, Acanthus mollis, Galtonia sp., Isotoma fluvatilis*, etc. Having said this I suppose the whole lot will turn to mush next winter. My point is, however, that further experimentation will increase our range of plants and add interest to our gardens. We may even find hardy strains of otherwise tender plants.

This year we had many visitors to the garden. I find showing the garden very difficult. People like Linc Foster (are there any others?) take you on a satisfying round trip with frequent stops at special plants, credible answers to a barrage of questions, good stories about plants, and a wealth of sound horticulture thrown in for good measure. I don't know how to lead a tour, forget names, fail to point out the plant the visitor brought last visit, and stand for minutes on end speechless in front of an unweeded disaster area. The sow thistle standing there about to discharge its seed over the whole bed has a hypnotic effect which drives names and aims out of one's mind. One stoops in embarrassment and idly starts weeding. But humiliation follows: instead of a weed it is a small alpine bun or possibly a branch from a daphne. The visitor is smiling and consoling. Too late the maxim is remembered: never weed in public. Also never apologize and never explain. As Lee Raden says, "Good gardeners don't see the weeds." Anyway weeds in a garden give it a human dimension, like a flaw in a Chinese vase. Who needs perfection?

The great satisfaction of weeding after Labor Day is that the ground seems to stay clear for the rest of the season. The oxalis and those two flat horrors euphorbia and purslane stop reappearing, and big plants like goldenrod and sow thistle, about to seed, are easier to pull. But insidiously chickweed reappears, dandelion and hawkweed form pretty rosettes that try to pass for *Oenothera caespitosa* and silene respectively. Weeds that grow through winter and early spring have an uncanny way of growing near a look-alike. As though they read the labels and pick a suitable one to colonize. We all know that chipmunks can read two words: crocus and tulipa.

But animals are another story. I oscillate between being a staunch member of the Bambi lobby, as Fred McGourty describes us, and being a wild-eyed potential killer of all forms of animal life. The destruction of bulbs, seeds, buds, leaves, roots, branches, and fruit seems malicious. Foot marks, holes, and burrows smack of vandalism. We need to remind ourselves constantly that we only share our land with the animals. If we really could eradicate every pest we would end up with a barren thing we wouldn't want—like a swimming pool or a parking lot—only good for unproductive exercise, or a wasteland of chemical poison like the lawns rich people are buying these days. Some compensations this fall: two wild turkeys crossing the garden with eight babies at full gobble, a fox strolling through the field opposite, beautiful pale-green snakes sliding through the thyme, bright-orange efts and grotesque toads under stones.

A Walk Around the Garden in Late Fall

WHAT A MAGNET the garden is, even in November and December. Last night there was a little snow. I am looking at it smugly from the kitchen after a leisurely breakfast. The thermometer reads 40 degrees. I know I cannot go outside. What luxury! The air is moist, and a pearl-grey mist hangs around the landscape. Soon a diffusion of sunlight glimmers through the grey: a challenge provoking me to action. I decide on a compromise. I change into Bean's rubber shoes, but no long-johns, just to take a quickie garden tour and smell the air.

What a difference between the first snow of the season and the last. By April the ground will be a weary tan with only a faint promise of viridian poking through the snow. In November the grass is a brilliant emerald green after a few soaking fall rains. The first snow comes as a threat, that winter will force us to change our routine, but it lacks the look of permanence that distinguishes January's thick blanket. The grass shines through it like Astroturf. The snow has started to melt now, and the tour is on. I bend down to pull a weed and find the ground cold and soggy. I decide to quit weeding until April. Kneeling is an invitation to soaked jeans and rheumatism.

I tell myself: what you can do is to clear the garden of all the things you don't want the snow to hide. Pick up the empty pots you left by the beds, the sticks and twigs from the last hurricane. Push the labels in deeper and remove the broken bits and pieces of plastic you left lying there until you could spare the time to decipher the washed-out names and replace them with legible, clean, whole labels. But it is really too late for that now. I haven't a clue as to where a new label would go.

Bring in the garden furniture. Bring in the concrete birdbath;

last time it was left outside it leaked. The cold frames have to be weighted down with logs and broken snowfence posts. Flat two-dimensional objects are easily airborne, and after a few severe storms, catches, hooks, and hinges are no longer reliable.

Another problem stares me in the eye: the leaves. To leave or not to leave, that is the question. The answer depends on next spring's good intentions. Leaves absolutely cannot be left on emerging bulb shoots. Yellow tulip and daffodil leaves look sick. On the other hand leaves have protective value for many plants. They have at least a neutral effect until March or April. But I found on Long Island, where a grove of bird cherry dropped limp, ugly leaves, and in Manhattan, where the tree of heaven shed its litter, that I had to remove every leaf by hand. Here in Massachusetts the maple leaves go brown and curly and retain a lot of air in their bulk, and not every leaf has to be raked up in November. But a sharp lookout for buried treasure is needed as soon as the snow finally goes. I may need to revise this theory next spring, but right now it is convenient.

I clean the garden of most of the trash and begin to wander around it for what seems like the first time since April, really taking a look at it. I fantasize about next spring's projects. I'll enlarge this bed a trifle, and this plant must be divided without fail. Here is a spreader I must move; it will soon engulf its neighbor. Here is a lithospermum I forgot to take into the cold frame. And look at this enormous, beautiful plant without a name tag. What could it be? Could it be . . . ? Is it . . . ? Yes, it is a mat of chickweed already the size of a large mossy sax. Practically while my back was turned! Quickly I rush to the barn to get a spade, a claw, and a bucket. I pull the chickweed and start on the sod I had just promised to remove next spring. I find more weeds to pull. Soon I forgot and kneel; my jeans are soaking. A sharp breeze blows up, and the temperature has risen to 45. I must go in.

But the garden is still irresistible. Those few visionary moments when I could conjure spring in all its glory make wet knees a fair price. I go upstairs to change. Downstairs again the mood has gone. The light is back to pearl grey, and I take down a new book on saxifrages.

Chores for Late Winter

A T THE START of another year, depending on your point
of view, you are either impatiently sitting out winter ach-
ing for spring, or living winter's tag-end to the full and wondering if you will be caught unprepared when spring finally
arrives. If you haven't already ordered seed go ahead and do
so. Also send for plant catalogs and order early to ensure getting
plants you want. Most nurseries run out of the one thing you
really wanted if you delay. And don't neglect to order your
quota of seed from the American Rock Garden Society seed
exchange. If you are a beginner, here is a short list of plants
which should be in everybody's garden and which you can be
fairly sure you will get if you order in reasonable time: *Dianthus
alpinus, Lewisia cotyledon, Lychnis flos-jovis, Arnica montana, Primula algida, Erinus alpinus, Draba aizoides, Erigeron compositus,
Gentian scabra, Aquilegia flabellata nana, Papaver alpinum.*

As soon as you get the seeds, fill a three-inch pot with Jiffymix, Promix, or a mixture of half coarse sand and half one
of the commercial soil-free mixes. Sow the seed if possible so
that the individual seeds are not closer than a quarter-inch apart,
but don't worry unduly if a few stick together—they are the
ones that will germinate. Don't feel you have to use up all the
seed in the packet; exchange your extras with a friend. Cover
the seed with a sprinkle of coarse sand. For large seed (pulsatilla
or muscari, for example) the sand might be an eighth of an inch
deep or more; for primulas, just a dusting. Water the pots by
standing them in a tray of water one to two inches deep. You
can let them soak all night, but an hour is usually enough. Put
the pots in a safe place outside but open to the weather. There
is no need to rush either germination or growth. If you have
the facilities you can grow the seeds under lights. This requires
careful watering both before and after germination, as the heat
of the lights dries the pots. If you want to take a midway course,
but each pot in a plastic bag and keep them in a garage or
unheated porch. After a week you will have to look at the pots
nearly every day to see if any have germinated. Take off the
bag to give more light when you notice the first green. After
germination it is a good idea to protect the pots from freezing
up again and to keep the seedlings growing. If you can't give

this much attention to your seedlings, better not try for early germination. Nature does quite a good job outdoors. On the other hand you miss a lot of fun seeing the plants develop while winter is dragging on. You could use a sunny window, but watch for dying, burning, drowning, and straining towards insufficient light.

Bring the bulbs from the cold frame in February if they are not frozen in, and gently force them. Where I live you don't gain much advantage by doing this, but you get to see the flowers at close quarters. By now the catalogs from Siskiyou, Daystar, Stonecrop, Russell Graham, Rocknoll, WeDu, Lamb, Rice Creek, and Eco Gardens should be on hand. When you specify the delivery date think about whether you are equipped to handle the plants on arrival. If the only place you can put them is in the ground, ask for a May delivery. I have lost a lot of plants by having to plant out in the cold soil of April. Better than immediate planting out is to plant them in pots until they have recovered from the voyage. That way, you can treat them like the invalids they often are.

If you have a period without snow, look for snowdrops and early crocuses in the garden and clean off dead leaves by hand or by using a flexible metal rake. If frost has left the ground, you may be tempted to work in the soil, but this is usually a poor idea. Most soils cannot be dug or cultivated this early, as wet soil is easily compacted. Be content to clean up and maybe prune a little if the urge to do something outdoors overtakes you. We who live in the frozen north usually have to wait until April, and even on Long Island early March is too soon to be messing around in the dirt.

Spring to me is when the grass along the highways turns green. Along one Connecticut east–west route, Interstate 84, this is usually around March 21, but green comes a week earlier along a state parkway forty miles south, and a week later on an east–west road forty miles north. "Usually" hardly ever happens, however, and each spring is different. If the ground does thaw in early March, how about digging some plants for the March plant show? A week or so potted in a cold frame or other protected area will bring drabas and androsaces into bloom.

Still Winter

"MARCH BRINGS BREEZES loud and shrill, stirs the dancing daffodil." Not usually true in New England. In New York City and on Long Island the early ones such as "Little Beauty" and "February Gold" could be out in late March, but snowdrops, crocus, *Scilla tubergeniana, Anemone blanda, Tulipa biflora,* and *T. kaufmanniana* are more reliable March bloomers. Farther north the tulips would hold back until the first warm spell in April, and in Massachusetts one is lucky to get even *Iris histrioides* in March. The first robin appears mid-month, and the Canada geese are using the same histrionics to gladden our hearts in spring that successfully brought sighs in the fall. The raccoon is out again, and the red squirrels vacate the bird feeders and head north.

There is a lot to look for in the garden but not much to see, unless you know where and how to look. It is a good time to get the labels back if you can find the pieces. The rule seems to be that if there is a plant there is no label, and vice versa. The deer have probably been celebrating the end of winter too. Press the plants that seem to have been kicked out back in place, and use as cuttings the partially munched primulas and douglasias. You have to be philosophic about the damage—perhaps it helps to know that every garden suffers its share of animal depredation. In Hempstead it used to be the immature male of *Homo sapiens* that stomped and broke labels. Take a cultivator and scratch out the footprints. Also plan to eliminate more of the lawn this year. You can steal five or six inches every year by edging. March is not the best time to dig up the sod, but it is a good time to dig through so that when the soil dries a little the sod comes up easily.

A lot of the seeds you sowed should be sprouting by now, especially if you had any indoors. If you sowed any annuals they could be large enough to transplant. Many people like to let the planting medium become quite dry so that when the pot is turned upside down and the contents slide out gently, the seedlings separate easily without damaging the roots. Root damage is the thing to avoid. After the seedling is planted in fresh compost a thorough soak is in order. My own method would be a little different, especially if the seedlings were very few or very many in the pot. With only two or three seedlings to transplant I try to separate the contents without disturbing the roots at all. This means the compost has to hold together and must not be really dry. In the other case, when the seed was sown thickly and separation into single tiny plants becomes nearly impossible (especially true of meconopsis and the like), I gently pull apart the compost into small clumps of seedlings and pot them up as I would a single plant. Curiously enough these clumps seem to develop better than single tiny plants do, and they can be transplanted again later in the season. It is *not* a good idea to leave a pot of overcrowded seedlings for a long period. The compost you use to transplant into could be the same mixture used for sowing—that is, for example, half Jiffymix and half coarse sand. Avoid using actual soil in the mix unless it has been sterilized, and be sure you have a strong stomach before you do much baking of soil in the kitchen stove; it's not a nice smell. Also consult a better authority than I for cooking times and temperatures.

LINNAEA BOREALIS, *a creeper for the woodland.*

PHLOX 'CHATTAHOOCHEE.' *This plant was originally found in Florida, but it is hardy much further north.*

⤳§ II §⤳

Random Species of the Garden

Perennials

WHAT A LOADED word! We use it in several contexts, some less neutral than others. If you are an alpine gardener you dismiss any largish plant as "just a perennial," meaning you don't have room for it. Or you turn around and say of a small bun that it is a "first-rate perennial," meaning that it lives more than one year. There are three ideas buried in the word: the first use is to contrast with an annual or a biennial. An annual flowers, makes seed, and dies in one season, a biennial uses the first season to make a rosette, then flowers, seeds, and dies the following year. There are other modes of growth which muddy these simple prototypes, but a true perennial ought to live a good long time to qualify for the name.

The second usage of the word contrasts a class of plants that contribute to a perennial border as distinct from a shrub border, a rock garden, a wild garden, or a "bedding-out" arrangement. You don't actually apply the word "perennial" to the biennials and annuals used to fill the gaps in a perennial border, but the sweep of the hand that indicates where the perennial border is doesn't offer the qualification that some of the plants are there under false pretenses. This would also be close to making "perennial" stand for "herbaceous perennial." That is, a plant which does not make any woody material. This would include both deciduous perennials (delphiniums) and evergreen perennials (sedums). These distinctions don't seem to matter in the rock garden; we never talk about a "mixed" planting just because it includes *Penstemon davidsonii* (shrubby), *Penstemon nitidus* (evergreen, and *Campanula raineri* (deciduous).

The third way you might use "perennial" is to mean "there every year." Then we would have to include annuals that self-sowed reliably but exclude monocarpic plants of whatever duration that didn't. Some plants are perennial in every sense. Take *Iris sibirica* for instance. Fit only for the border, reliably hardy and long lived, impossible to eradicate once happily established, it has all the hallmarks of perennialdom. It was one of the first plants I rushed to buy, one of the first plants whose varieties and forms I wanted to collect, and one of the first plants I wanted to get rid of. But no amount of digging, hacking, and hauling bushel baskets to the compost heap will rid you of these beautiful plants. The seedlings are everywhere, and the seed doesn't mind spending a year or so in the compost heap preparing to sneak back into the garden again. Alongside *Iris sibirica* I would place echinops; most border campanulas but especially *C. persicifolia*, *C. glomerata*, and *C. latifolia*; many large composites such as heliopsis and coreopis; and hosts of others as being perennial in every sense.

Perennial in the "always-there" sense are digitalis, verbascums, *Stachys lanata*, *Calceolaria mexicana*, and a crowd of large silenes. If these are annuals or biennials they produce an unfailing supply of volunteers. Some of them are only borderline welcome, but all are showy and cheerful. It is hard to call them weeds when they flower. They are like garrulous neighbors who bring the news and gossip you long for but try your patience as you perpetually fail to get them to leave when they have outstayed their welcome. Included amongst these tyrants are the established annuals such as nigella, larkspur, and Johnny-jump-ups. You can always get rid of a single plant by being rude, but they have two strategic weapons, ubiquity and a beauty, that only a philistine would want to destroy.

But what can we call the alpines that die each year or are so transitory that we never seem to be able to establish them? *Dianthus alpinus*, *Physoplexis comosa*, *Silene hookeri* . . . those choice plants that I try year after year and that frequently flower but never keep for long. And if they seem "easy" at first I must collect seed to be sure that I have a sporting chance of having them again. Include *Dianthus callizonus*, *Campanula raineri*, *Hymenoxys grandiflora*, *Androsace carnea*, and so on. Sometimes I think I "have" them, but none of them are in the *Echinops sphaerocephalus* class of haveness, where seed has permeated every compost heap and lies dormant in every bed waiting to germinate and send forth the greyish-white heads that attract every bee in Massachusetts. I have never had a problem with too much *Androsace ciliata* or *Douglasia nivalis*. In fact, using both words loosely, they could be described as "tender annuals." Tender, because they are not heartily hardy [too delicate to withstand a muggy July or an open January]; annual, because they live for only one year. They sometimes don't even bother setting seed, so you can't in fairness call them monocarpic.

And are crocus, tricyrtis, and lilium perennial? They honestly try to be, but the animals see to it that their life-span is short, and they can at best be described as impermanent. And if they are impermanent they really can't be described as perennial, can they? And what about tulips? Even if you protect them with chicken wire and mothballs they seem to decrease each year until you are left with a few single leaves that come from minuscule non-flowering bulbs that have pulled themselves so far down into the soil that there is nothing you can do to get them out. Perennial? I'd call them weeds, non-flowering weeds.

Recently a Czech gardener visited us for two days and constructed a crevice garden. He claims, and this still has to be tested, that many alpines, if transplanted, are monocarpic—specifically *Dianthus alpinus* and *Physoplexis comosa*. These, Czech claims, can only be grown from seed sown in situ if they are to be perennial. Well, I can try, since he made the crevice garden, but I remain very sceptical until these theories have been tested. Maybe all those "perennials" that turn out to be "annual," "biennial," or "short-lived perennial" will turn out, in the crevice garden, to be the weedy perennials I want them to be.

The Crème de la Crème

A S YOU GET deeper and deeper into alpines, reading books and journals, talking to the cognoscenti, seeing slides, and attending conferences, you begin to take in the fact that a number of plant names crop up time and time again. Eventually you also realize that it is "everybody's" aim to grow these plants. It is one of the rites of passage to have tried and either failed completely or succeeded partially. If you succeed you join the Blessed in Valhalla or Olympus—your choice. Ordinary folk have a few partial successes and more failures. But then they can talk about these plants with at least the authority of a failed Ph.D. If you haven't tried any of them, you haven't received the call. Perhaps you need psychotherapy or have an acute case of sour grapes.

There are those wonderful plants we only ever see on slides

AQUILEGIA JONESII, *a difficult Rocky Mountain columbine.*

at international conferences. They are usually from South America, Mount Kilimanjaro, Iran, or the less reliable parts of the Himalayas. They are introduced to us by an explorer or a botanist. The indomitable and incomprehensible unveil the unobtainable and ungrowable. Usually you see the pictures just once; there is a breathy sound as a hundred people suck in air with amazement and envy. Then the plants recede into total obscurity. You never see them or hear of them again. The rosulate violas, the Himalayan saxifrages, the dionysias, the rare eriogonums, and more and more. These are *not* the plants I mean.

Then there are the other wonderful plants that you see on the show benches of England. Plants to covet, find, and try to grow. They are the plants you can sometimes buy in a backyard in Huddersfield or that one and only one nurseryman has propagated and doesn't have enough to list. Or one of the Blessed has one to spare but only for exchange, and all you have to exchange is a cutting from a phlox whose label got lost. Often the plant is a rare form or a hybrid that was "found in so-an-so's garden" (was it lost?). Occasionally a plant is sneaked into the United States and propagated for a short time before vanishing from sight. If somebody in the U.S. succeeds in making it happy we can even see it on the show bench here. If it is a

North American native, change all these locations. Sometimes seed is sent by a friend in Czechoslovakia or the Archibalds collect it in Greece and list it tagged "small quantities only."

Well, I have tried these plants and mostly failed. Here is a list of partial confession. The whole truth would be too depressing.

Eritrichium nanum. This has to head the list. Nobody gets to Valhalla on this one. I have tried it indoors, in beds with and without winter protection, and in containers. The closest I have been to the Grail is one flower on one plant. They can be brought through one winter without an unduly large number of losses, but two is one too many. Ellie Spingarn and Lee Raden have both flowered it, but neither has kept it long as far as I know. Lee's methods involve a constant stream of air directed over the plants. Fred Watson was able to root several cuttings in sand.

Physoplexis comosa. I grew several and flowered two one year and one another. None remain of these. This year I am again growing them, this time in containers. This is a plant that many people can grow well, judging by the frequency with which seed is offered in the seedlists. Once you have seen an example of these quaint flowers you too will get the bug. Unless your heart is quite cold.

Androsace helvetica. Everybody has seen the photograph of this plant growing in the wild in Anna Griffith's book. It is the epitome of alpine-plant grace, posture, and location. I have had some success with many other androsaces, but this one is much harder to obtain and, I assume, to grow.

Campanula piperi. The gem from the Pacific Northwest. Seed is sometimes offered in the American Rock Garden Society's seedlist, usually collected, because I think this is hard to cultivate. I have had flowers twice but no rerun and no seed. There are a number of difficult campanulas such as *C. zoysii,* and *C. incisa,* and different people find others difficult. It is not a matter for too much mourning since there are plenty of first-rate campanulas of equal value to the toughies. It is the challenge that gets to you.

Primula allionii. This shouldn't be included, because many people grow this plant and several exquisite forms in their alpine houses. Roxy Gevjan comes to mind in the U.S. and Kath

Dryden in the U.K.; both have mastered its cultivation. My inclusion of *P. allionii* stems from a visit to Hartside Nursery in England where I saw it growing outside. My aim is to do the same. I thought I had succeeded when I had a plant this year covered with blossoms and in fine shape. I now think this is a hybrid and not the species. However I am still trying.

Aquilegia jonesii. Seed is available, it germinates, we get plants, they die. If they don't die, they don't flower. Occasionally, one will flower and then die.

Saxifraga longifolia. This is monocarpic; after flowering it dies. It is grown for the circular pad of stiff, grey leaves encrusted with dots of lime. You can wait five years for the flower which rises in a stately column then curves over as it triumphantly matures to a magnificent plume of white flowers, as much as two feet in height. Cultivation can be considered successful if you get viable seed or self-sown seedlings.

Dicentra peregrina. According to Ev Whittemore this is easy. It self-sows in scree in North Carolina. Norman Singer grew a plant to perfection until visited by a pundit from Japan who strongly advised fertilizing. The plant then died. I think a number of others have grown it successfully. The best I have had is a few leaves which go dormant quicker than a groundhog in February. But surely, seed has to be fresher than seedlist seed.

Draba mollissima. This is getting one more try. I will not grow plants that depend entirely on alpine housework. Draba m. suffers indoors in my care. Outside it has so far been a total loss. I now have a batch of seedlings which I am giving a chance to redeem the species. Again there are a number of drabas of almost equal value that will tolerate raised beds. I thought *D. polytricha* was willing, but I now have doubts about that one, too. *D. rosularia* may have to do as a stand-in.

Corydalis cashmeriana. There are a number of plants, another is *Leucocrinum montanum*, which arrive as tiny bulbs or tubers; you plant them in October and never hear another word. This happens no matter where you put them, indoors or out.

Calceolaria darwinii. This is another siren from Anna Griffith. It can be grown. The Bevingtons grow it in England. I have not seen it in the U.S. yet. I would like to grow this, even indoors, just once. If it insists on indoors, however, I will say good-bye. Promise.

Viola beckwithii. Since Jerry Colly of Siskiyou Nursery propagates it and sells it, there must be a way of growing it by ordinary mortals. What do you do with those long roots when the plants arrive in April?

Celmisia sessiliflora. I would also coddle this New Zealander if I could get it going at all. Celmisia seed is reluctant to germinate. I saw great celmisias in Hugh Barr's garden and in Dilys Davies's garden last October in the Lake District, but that probably means they are Zone 7 instead of Zone 5. Fred Watson grows celmisias in New Hampshire but not entirely in the open air. They spend the winter either indoors or under one of his A-frame erectibles. With heat? I don't know. *C. sessiliflora* doesn't have the best leaves, but it is relatively flat and might be protectable in a raised bed.

Kelseya uniflora. This was grown by Joan Means from a cutting. But for how long? I brought seed back from the Big Horns in Montana, and it germinated, but the seedlings succumbed during the summer. Very little seed is passed around. Winter probably descends rather rapidly on the Big Horn, and we were lucky to get seed before the snow came.

Lupinus lepidus v. lobbii. Very tantalizing. I have had flowers on many of the dwarf western lupins but no success at keeping them going. The seed they produce usually isn't viable, and either the plants are short lived or they resent my accommodations.

Douglasia montana. Why is this plant so much more obstinate than *D. nivalis* or *Vitaliana primulaeflora*? People in Washington State talk about *D. laevigata* as the "easy one," but for me this is almost as difficult as *D. montana*.

The list could go on and on; many primulas belong here and a few composites. I hope the point is made, though, that far from wishing to discourage you from growing the *crème de la crème*, I want to invite you to join the happy band of failures. Better to have loved and lost!

Auriculas

THERE ARE SEVERAL meanings to the word *auricula*. To examine them we have to go back to the genus *Primula*.

A species is a collection of plants which are alike enough botanically so that we can say they are the "same thing." A genus is a collection of species which have botanical similarities. The genus *Primula* contains an enormous number of species; so many (more than five hundred) that in order to think about them effectively taxonomists have divided them up into sections. At one time there were thirty sections of primulas. Each section could be thought of as a subgenus, but that would not be currently botanically correct, though the difference between subgenus and section escapes me. What in fact has happened is that there are now seven subgenera of primulas, each of which is subdivided into sections—twenty-one sections in all. It is convenient for gardeners to take note of and remember a few of the sections, since the grouping tells something about the horticultural needs of the species in that section. For instance the Candelabra section likes moisture. They are also relatively tall and look best grouped in a congenial location near a stream. The border is not the best place for Candelabra primulas, but the easier ones would be tolerant. The rock-garden scree is the wrong place, and you would only grow a Candelabra there as an experiment, in order to look at a specimen for one season, not with any real hope of success. This section includes *Primula japonica*, *P. bulleyana*, and *P. cockburniana*, and many others mostly from Asia.

Another section of the genus *Primula* is the Auricula section. There is now a subgenus *Auriculastrum* with Auricula as a section. This section is mostly European, and the species in it are mostly alpines. Many of them are red–deep pink–magenta, most are medium sized, and nearly all of them have leathery leaves different from the crinkly leaves of the familiar primroses (*P. vulgaris*) and the Polyanthus types (these last belong to the Vernales section). There is great diversity amongst the species of the Auricula section, so generalizations are deceptive. For instance the small *P. minima*, the sticky *P. viscosa*, and the violet *P. marginata* all belong to the Auricula section.

One particular member of the section is the species *Primula auricula*, giving us the second usage of the word. This is a handsome alpine plant with clear yellow flowers and medium height (i.e., it is not creeping and not Candelabra tall). About six inches would be an average height. The plant is widespread and found in the wild in France, Switzerland, Austria, and Czechoslovakia, usually on limestone.

The species *P. auricula* hybridizes in the wild with other members of the Auricula section, in particular *P. hirsuta* (also known as *P. rubra*). This cross has been given the name *P.X pubescens*. But gardeners have crossed *P. auricula* not only with *P. hirsuta* but with other species such as *P. viscosa*. The results of these crosses and subsequent selection have given us a great variety of forms including many beautiful plants and of course some doubles. Some have been propagated vegetatively by cuttings and offsets and given names. A few well-known clones are "Rufus" and "Lady Daresbury." Marge Walsh of Daystar nursery usually has a good selection. Run-of-the-mill crosses have also been grown in borders; these are called Border Auriculas and are sold without names in garden centers. They have sometimes been grown from a good strain of seed, such as the Douglas strain. These have interesting, dusky colors—plum, brown, bronze—and the plants have the leathery leaves characteristic of *P. auricula*. They are less flashy than Polyanthus and *P. vulgaris*, but many people prefer the subtle colors. In my experience they do not flower as profusely as primulas from the Vernales section, and this may also account for their lesser popularity.

A fourth meaning attached to *auricula* has arisen because the hybrids of *P. auricula* and *P. hirsuta* have been highly bred since the eighteenth century for certain characteristics of the flowers. Especially for the *farina*, which is a feature of many species of the genus *Primula*. Farina is a light-colored powdery substance occurring on the plants. One section of the genus, the Farinosae, is so named because many of the species in the section have farina on their flowers, stems, or leaves. One member of this section is called *P. auriculata* just to add to the confusion. The location of the farina of interest to the eighteenth-century breeders was on the flowers themselves, mostly a band of farina surrounding the eye. A mutation apparently caused the edges

PRIMULA MARGINATA, *an Auricula primula from
the European Alps.*

of some flowers to be green or grey as though petal and leaf had become confused. This feature was also developed as part of the breeding program. What was "natural" and what "man-made" is not so important as the fact that these plants became the sport of a large number of gardeners over the centuries. Their products are not garden plants, because their beauty is easily marred by rain. There exists a whole population of clones and strains of highly bred Auriculas which are grown in cool greenhouses. The standards of beauty are very refined, and of least importance are the shape, texture, and color of the leaf. Of very little importance is the sturdiness of the plant, and of utmost importance are the color and design of the flower and the distribution of farina, or "paste," as it is called. It is worth noting that a flower whose pistil is visible could never appear on the showbench. Another quirky rule is that there should be an odd number of pips on the truss. These criteria are of no significance at all for an ordinary gardener. The rejects of the Auricula showmen could be very beautiful plants, but like the offspring of some mixed marriages, they are suitable neither for the garden nor the show bench. The Auricula people have further confused the name game by dividing Auriculas into Show Auriculas and Alpine Auriculas according to whether they have farina or have not. Other classifications take into account body color and what color the edge is. The Alpine Auriculas have nothing to do with either *Primula auricula* or the Alps, except insofar as the species is part of their ancestry. They are as far from the Alps genetically, aesthetically, and horticulturally as it is possible to be. Even narcissus is not more overbred.

So we have these uses: Auricula, the show plant; Auriculas, border plants (= *P.X pubescens*); Auricula hybrids, named clones; *Primula auricula*, the species; and Auricula section of the genus *Primula* (subgenus *Auriculastrum*).

A Final Word on Auriculas

They said, "What are you thinking
When you talk about auricula?"
Without so much as blinking
He said "Nothing in particular."

"And should we say 'Auricula'
Or stick to cross pubescens?"
He spoke in accents secular:
"Observe the inflorescence."

They asked about farina
And is Auricula specific?
He kept his bright demeanor
And said, "They're *all* terrific!"

"Auricula means primula
We gather from your discourse."
"Not quite, but it's as similar
As Pony is to Horse."

Androsaces

T O LEARN MORE about this glorious genus you should read
Smith and Lowe's monograph published by the Alpine
Garden Society. Not everyone thinks these plants are glorious;
other epithets might be: too small to be of any value, irritatingly
unpredictable, colorless and inconsequential, of snob value only,
too difficult for me. As with all such value judgments there is
an element of truth in these complaints, and the purpose of this
note is to advise beginners what is worth trying among androsaces. I shall stop short of giving advice for experts; rather I
would ask for theirs on taking care of the prima donnas that
many of us long to grow to the perfection that some of the
British have achieved in their alpine houses.

An overview of the genus *Androsace* might be useful if only
to point out that there are androsaces that everyone can grow
and some that nobody can grow. There are essentially three
kinds. The first are annuals, although they behave like biennials.
They grow from seed sown, let's say, in February into plants
big enough to plant out in the garden by August. Very rarely
they will flower the first year, but mostly they wait until the
next spring. After flowering some of them proceed to make
themselves at home by shedding thousands of seeds which will

grow into plants flowering the following spring. Others will make plenty of seed but not self-sow, and you need to collect the seed and repeat the process for next year's plants.

The books all say these "annual" androsaces are worthless for the rock garden. This is false. There are a number of rather indifferent plants if you take them individually, but a mass of them can be quite effective, especially with scillas, for instance, growing amongst them. These androsaces have the airiness of a small gypsophila, the only caveat being that if the flowers are very small you should get rid of them before they spread too far. I would like to name and describe individual species in this group, but the names of the seeds you get from the exchanges are not reliable. The three names most often met with are *Androsace lactiflora, A. septentrionalis,* and *A. chaixii.* Any of these is likely to give you plants about six inches tall or more, growing from a single rosette of narrowish, slightly toothed leaves. At the top of the stem is a rather loose umbel of white flowers, the individual flowers being about a quarter-inch across. *A. chaixii* is described as rose, but I have had nothing but white.

The name to avoid amongst the "annual" androsaces, unless you are a collector, is *A. maxima,* which has flowers so reduced in size that it depends for its interest on the green calyx, so in fact it looks as though the flowers just fell off. Even this plant is not totally without charm, though. Another member of this group, in the Andraspis section, is *A. albana,* which is definitely worth growing. I haven't had it self-sow, and it can hardly be claimed to be a nuisance. The leaves are thick and undulate attractively, and the rosette can develop into a group of huddled rosettes. The stems are rather thick and stiff, but the flowers are more substantial than those of the other members of the section and can bloom on and off all through the year. I would recommend to anybody with a spark of curiosity that he try any androsace from this section; as long as he remembers to be on the lookout for a possible weed. Place these androsaces with your second-best plants, not with tiny jewels.

The second group of androsaces is also quite easy for the most part. This is the Chamaejasme section. They tend to run and form mats of plants, sometimes by making strawberrylike runners. The one everybody should grow is the familiar *A. sar-mentosa*. This is sometimes confused with *A. primuloides*, the two being either identical or so similar it doesn't matter. There are a number of forms going around, but no name will guarantee a particular form. I have grown plants with names like *chumbyi*, *watkinsonii*, and *yunnanensis*; you may get something different from what you already have, but don't rely on it. The variations are in tightness of the mat and rosettes, height of the flowering stem, depth of pink, and size of the flower. I haven't had an unattractive form. Propagation is easy by rooting a rosette, so it is better to buy a plant from a nursery than to grow from seed, on the theory that the nursery had the gumption to select a good form to sell. These plants need room to spread; they are not as vigorous as *Phlox subulata* or *Arabis caucasica* but will grow as fast as *Gypsophila repens*. If you enjoy playing around with plant associations and color combinations this is the kind of reliable alpine that lends itself to artistic arrangements, shaping itself over rocks as a bonus where needed.

Two similar but more refined Chamaejasme androsaces are *A. sempervivoides*, which has tight rosettes and pink flowers and is not so easy to establish, and *A. chamaejasme*, which has hairs on leaf margin and white flowers. The yellow eye turns pink with age, and you get a multicolored effect on one plant. This is not nearly as easy as *A. sarmentosa*, but it's one to try in a well-chosen spot in the rock garden or to plant in a container where it will be well behaved for a few years.

In the same section is *Androsace lanuginosa*, which is the same plant as *A. occulata*. This blooms later than most androsaces. Its attractive feature is the hairiness of the leaves, which give the impression of being silver rather than grey. The flowers are attractive too, but they don't cover the mats usually and are a pale enough pink so that the impact is gentler than with *A. sarmentosa*. The stems are long but only root down occasionally, unlike sarmentosa which roots often and forms rosettes. The blooming period is longer too, and you may find a campanula to keep *A. lanuginosa* company; how about *C. cochlearifolia? C. rotundifolia* might swamp it.

There are other androsaces in the Chamaejasme section. *A.*

spinulifera and *A. strigilosa* are described as rather similar, but all the plants I have grown with those names have been in the Andraspis section. If you get a chance go ahead and try them for yourself. One plant I have had and kept going only by collecting seed is *A. aizoon coccinea* (also known as *bulleyana*). This is a delicious strawberry-ice-cream color—roughly, deep scarlet. The plant is a wee bit straggly, but the color is great. Smith and Lowe describe it as "lost to cultivation," but it has appeared in the seedlists within the last five years, so look out for it.

Another prize is *A. villosa*. If you can get seed of this very special plant, and if it germinates, and if you get a transplant big enough to plant out in August, either choose a raised bed with good drainage or plant it in a container so that you can keep winter rains off the leaves. But don't be afraid of it; it is fairly difficult but not impossible for a gardener with a little experience (i.e., acquired common sense).

The third group of androsaces is the Aretia section, the aretian androsaces. These are the plants which give the genus its mystique, scaring off beginners and making plant snobs of anyone who manages to keep a couple of species alive for more than a year. Starting with the easiest we get *Androsace lactaea* and *A. carnea*. (I have seen these placed in the previous section.) These are fairly similar except that the stalks of *lactaea* are longer, making the umbel at the top of the stem less tight and not as pretty. Also, while *lactaea* is always white, *carnea* has some elegant short forms and deep colors and on the average gives us better plants. I cannot keep track of the names of these subspecies and varieties. The leaves of the rosettes are more or less pointed and more or less narrow, and the flower stems are two to four inches tall. Grow any or all forms and give them as good a place as you can spare in a raised bed or container. Don't be surprised if you lose them after a couple of years, and always collect seed to keep new plants coming on to replace the losses. Ultimately you may find the right conditions for permanence, and then you will be a rock gardener. *A. hedraeantha* and *A. mathildae* are in the same league. Everybody should try them, and most people will succeed some of the time. *A. mathildae* is a tiny, half-inch-high pixy with glossy leaves.

The more difficult members of the Aretia section can be left until you really have the androsace bug. Expect disappointment, but when you finally do succeed you will get a tremendous amount of pleasure from flowering them even if they don't manage two years in a row. The names to look for are *A. vandellii (=imbricata)*, which is hairy with silver leaves; *A. hirtella; A. cylindrica* (little cylinders of old leaves); and *A. hausmannii* (fleshy, wedgy leaves). These are all white-flowered treasures which a few brilliant gardeners can coax into making mats six inches across, though most of us cannot do this. *A. pyrenaica* and *A. helvetica* are met with less often; you really need to know somebody growing them in order to get seed. There are two pink-flowered plants which are well worth looking for: *Androsace ciliata* (not hairy) is a really beautiful bun, not easy but easier than most of the above. There is also a hybrid of *carnea X pyrenaica* which is a very good plant that you can sometimes buy as a plant. I believe it comes true from seed, and I believe it is the plant called "Millstream" because the cross was made by Linc Foster. It has small green leaves and plenty of good pink flowers—a better looking plant than *A. carnea* and easier than *A. pyrenaica*.

If you want to identify plants expertly, you should spend a lot of time surreptitiously reading labels, until you feel confident about the names. The botanical features that help (mostly shape and location of tiny hairs) need a magnifying glass, patience, and the eyesight of youth.

There are many androsaces not yet mentioned, including a whole section of slightly tender plants that are closer to primulas and want woodland conditions. There are names from the Himalayas never found in lists. Other names I have found in lists and tried include *A. macrantha, spinulifera, pedemontana, elongata, filiformis, foliosa, kochii, libanotica, mariae, pubescens, rotundifolia, taurica, turczaniowii,* and *barbulata*. They have turned out to be non-viable, tender, or annual and unmemorable. No advice, however should discourage you from trying any and all from seed if you want adventure and the hope of ethereal beauty.

Douglasias are New World androsaces; sometimes they are

lumped with the androsaces. They appear to retain their separate identity as a geopolitical gesture. *Vitaliana* is a European doug-lasia with similar reasons for separation. Anyway they are all great plants and should be grown with the best androsaces. *Vitaliana primulaeflora* is the easiest, a tight mat which grows appreciably each year but doesn't ramp and covers itself with butter-yellow flowers in early spring. Its only misfortune is to bloom with the drabas and to get lost in the surge of yellow that sweeps over the garden in late April.

The douglasias are not so accommodating, and you should always collect seed and resow. I have found *Douglasia nivalis* to be one of the best; it has greyish, needle-looking leaves, but they are neither sharp nor stiff. The flowers are pink, and the total effect is spectacular. *D. laevigata* is similar to *Androsace ciliata*. Both this and *D. montana*, from the Cascades, are desir-able and temperamental.

Whenever you get seed of androsace sow it right away. I tend to treat all seed alike, but with androsaces I usually add a little extra coarse sand; the drainage has to be good but more im-portant is the fact that germination is very erratic. All pots should be kept at least two seasons. If you keep a peaty mixture longer than half a year it tends to pack down, and the seedlings that do sprout seem to lack vigor. If you get a couple of seedlings in a pot don't be in a hurry to transplant. Try to separate the seedlings so that none of the original mixture is lost or disturbed, for there may be another seed in there that could germinate in a month or so. Of course if you have plenty of seedlings such care is unnecessary, and none of this fuss applies to the annual types. You wouldn't even save the pot a second year.

One problem with complex genera like the androsaces is growing seed with new and unlisted names: shall I keep it or dump it? Usually they fail to germinate or turn out to be close relatives of *A. lactiflora or A. albana*. Androsaces are members of the Primula family, and there is a family resemblance to *Primula angustifolia*, *Primula scotica*, and the smaller birds-eye primulas. Treat them as mountain plants, not as woodlanders— no deep shade. I think *A. sarmentosa* will suffer a little shade, but all the others need sun. On the other hand they do not seem to like hot mid-day midsummer sun, and they hate muggy weather, so find a place on the cool side of a slope or where tree shade strikes at mid-day, or move your containers around until you find the best location. When you find the right location tell your friends. We are all trying to get androsaces to thrive. They are the epitome of alpine gardening. A good plant of *Androsace vandellii* will raise your self-esteem several notches, and a mat of *A. sarmentosa* will raise your spirits and nudge your relatives and friends closer to understanding your passion—as if you cared.

Crucifers

C AN YOU REMEMBER your first positive experience of rock-garden plants? We didn't have a rock garden when I was young; the closest we came was a large ceramic drainpipe sporting a mossy saxifrage. But long after leaving home I would return on summer visits and observe with great admiration the rockery of a neighbor. This was a tiny plot barely fifteen by thirty feet and so steep as to be almost a wall. Each summer it was covered with aubrieta, alyssum, and arabis. There were other things growing there too, but these three seemed to predominate, and they struck a chord that has never stopped reverberating.

Three crucifers. They are in everybody's garden and frowned on for their exuberance—they are really unfit for more genteel company. But they exemplify one characteristic that most alpines share: they are *strictly* plants that belong in a garden; you would never pick them to put them in vases. In fact their ultimate effect is determined at the time you plant them. Under a tree they will straggle and pine, and once that happens they are almost unmovable, as I discovered when I tried to grow them in the canyons of New York City. But the same aubrieta, alyssum, and arabis were the first plants I bought when I finally got my own garden.

Since those early longings and failures I have discovered what the whole world knows about basket of gold, aubrieta, and arabis. First, they are members of the same botanical family,

Cruciferae, which includes a lot of vegetables and thousands of weeds. Second, they are each just one member of three genera within the family, and each genus contains many species worth growing. The name "crucifer" comes from the four petals evenly spaced like a cross. Another common name for the Cruciferae is the Mustard family, and an alternate botanical name is Brassicaceae.

On the way to finding out these elementary facts about the crucifers, I discovered candytuft and *Draba sibirica*, completing a quintet of reliable, hardy, and beautiful but very vigorous plants. They have such a reputation for heartiness, indeed, that most people don't look beyond them to find what other species in each genus are worth growing, so here is a brief rundown of some crucifers great and small, refined and weedy, difficult and easy.

Alyssum saxatilis (basket of gold, now *Aurinia saxatilis*) itself has several forms. There is the usual deep yellow, and *A. saxatilis citrina*, which is a lemon yellow. The yellows are reminiscent of forsythia color forms; you always want the other one than the one you have. But I really like both colors. There is a buff color too, usually given the name "Dudley Neville," but the plant is not very vigorous and is no improvement on the standard ones. There is also a double form which I have never succeeded in keeping, and "Dudley Neville" has a variegated leaf form. A different, more refined plant is the miniature *A. saxatile* "Tom Thumb," which doesn't flower as much but grows into a shrublike mound that doesn't need hacking back the way *A. saxatile* does. The other alyssums are plentiful, and you should certainly try a few of them from the seedlists.

A. cuneifolium is a little treasure, well behaved and quite perennial, forming a flat mat of small silver leaves. You get a few flowers in the first summer from seed sown in spring. *A. argenteum* is a big bushy plant which needs a lot of space and self-sows. In between these two are alyssums of varying heights and dispositions such as *A. moellendorfianum, A. repens, A. wulfenianum, A. rostratum,* and *A. tortuosum.* A few seem to be tender, such as *A. condensatum,* but all are worth a try. I think there must be some hybridizing in gardens or in the wild, as one batch of seed can give quite a bit of variation.

Close to Genus *Alyssum* is *Ptilotrichum*. The one that is easily obtainable is *P. spinosum*, which forms a very choice little bush with not very scary thorns. The flowers can be a dingy white or a luscious pink. Even the dingy white gives you a good plant; just place it where dingy is a plus.

Alyssoides graeca (= A. utriculata) sounds as though it should be like the genus *Alyssum*, but the flowers are inferior; you grow it for the fat pods in the late summer. The North American counterpart of the genus *Alyssum* is *Lesquerella*. Some of these appear in the seed exchanges, and you should try them all. I have had limited success; *Physaria* is also worth a shot. The leaves of these westerners are tantalizingly silver and grey.

Arabis caucasica also has some deviation from the standard white. Various pink forms exist, usually only the merest blush. One plant has double flowers, another, variegated leaves. Few other arabis are really choice plants; *A. ferdinandi-coburgii variegata* forms a pretty mat, and *A. X kellereri* is a nice bun. Some, like *A. soyeri*, are Plain Janes which send up long stalks with nothing much on them. *A. lyallii* and *A. sturii* are similar if not identical wandering mats with lots of flowers, but even they do not produce enough blooms, unless the form you have has especially large flowers. I have been searching for a good deep-pink arabis for a long time. I have sowed seed labeled *A. blepharophylla*, *A. verna*, and *A. cypria*, but they have all been the same rather coarse plant. This year a friend gave me the "true *A. blepharophylla*," so I am hoping spring will bring fulfillment.

Schivereckia podolica is like a very good small arabis, making an attractive grey mound when out of flower.

More refined than the arabises are the aubrietas. You can grow a whole range of color forms from seed of *A. deltoidea*; every commercial seed company has a strain or several. Or you can buy named clones. The names and descriptions are seductive, but I have found most of them hard to establish and not very vigorous. After buying every name from every catalog and bringing back a large number from England, I retain only one survivor, a variegated-leaf form which looks happy enough but hasn't gotten very big. Actually these fancy forms of crucifers seem to travel by mail very badly, often arriving as mush. Once you have one established you can increase your stock by cuttings.

Nothing has the impact of a brilliant double-purple aubrieta: English gardens in June have me drooling. Farrer dismisses species aubrietas in favor of these garden hybrids, but there are plenty of species worth growing. *A. columnea ssp. italica*, *A. intermedia*, *A. olympica*, *A. alpina*, *A. deltoidea leichtlinii*—all have personality without flamboyance.

Iberis have two beautiful features; their glossy dark-green leaves, and the brilliant white of their flowers. The big named forms of *Iberis sempervirens* are the plants you usually get in a nursery, and every garden needs a few of these showy bushes. There are smaller plants with some elegance. *I. saxatilis* and *I pygmaea* (is the second just a form?) can be placed with the choicest plants and look right. There are annual iberis, of course, descended from *I. amara* and *I. umbellata*, also biennial types such as *I. gibraltarica* (or this may be *I. jordanii* or *I. pruitii*). In any case the flowers on any of these may be tinged with, or quite deep, lilac. The biennials can make fairly large bushes which fade away for the winter leaving a bevy of babies for next spring.

This year I have *I. aurosica* and *I. spathulata*, which look promising too.

The genus *Aethionema* in seedlists is often unreliable, so keep trying various names until you get plants that you want to do some self-sowing. *A. pulchellum* and *A. grandiflora* are the names to go for. The plants to avoid have tiny pink flowers. Whatever you do don't let these ugly little weeds go to seed, or you will never be rid of them. One seedlist which should know better constantly sends out seeds labelled *A. creticum* and *A. graecum* which turn out to be "the weed." The plant called "Warley Rose" is a clone of *A. armenum*, but if you grow plants from seed with this name they are unlikely to be Rose's twin. If you do get a good aethionema sowing around, it will place itself very attractively in cracks and crevices. Ultimately, though, there will be too many, and you will face the heartbreaking job of pulling up these perfectly lovely plants. They end up on the compost heap since they can't be transplanted successfully.

The drabas are the earliest group of plants to bloom. *Draba sibirica* is the happy mat that glows in the April mud and always looks like the guest that arrived early; you want to be welcoming but aren't really ready. It belongs in the hurly-burly of the other mat formers and can hold its own even in part shade. There are many, many drabas—too many. A few are amongst the choicest treasures, like *D. bryoides* (also known as *imbricata*), and some are beautiful little buns like *D. aizoides* and its many look-alikes. They self-sow into a charming bunnery until there isn't a single plant whose name you are really sure of. Some of them are quite tender like *D. mollissima* and need protective care. But many, alas, are hideous white weeds fit for nowhere except the Employees Only section of a botanical garden. There is much to be said for drabas, and if you can ruthlessly reject the uglies there is a lot of fun to had growing twenty species or so each year for three or four years. The good white ones are *D. dedeana* and *D. fladnyzensis*; grow any others with great circumspection. Also, grow nothing from Japan. Greece and Turkey have some of the best soft grey-green buns.

Another early bird is the genus *Thlaspi*. *T. bellidifolium* and *T. rotundifolium* are good ones with purplish flowers and typical "pennycress" leaves. *T. bulbosum* is also mauve. The white thlaspis are not so attractive, but a few are worth having around, such as *T. montanum* and *T. alpinum*. Just don't let them take over, even if you do like their neat rosettes.

The last big group of crucifers for the rock garden are the wallflowers—Genus *Erysimum* and Genus *Cheiranthus*. A characteristic of many crucifers is the way the stems elongate as the fruit forms. Sometimes the pod is the only attractive aspect (*Fibigia* and *Lunaria*), and sometimes the plant, after it loses the freshness of the first flowers, begins to look gawky and uncomfortable like a half-dressed man getting out of formal clothes. The wallflowers can be particularly coarse looking in middle age, but nearly all are worth growing for their first week or so in full beauty.

Cheiranthus allionii, the "Siberian" wallflower, is yellow, and the "English" wallflowers are biennials and only useful for group plantings in English cities or scattered around those extravaganzas people call "cottage gardens." The flowers are usually brown or colors pretty close to brown.

Erysimum amoenum is a lovely purplish-pink wallflower from the Rockies. It can also be yellow. *E. nivale* is a yellow one found on Loveland Pass and elsewhere in Colorado. The best European is *E. helveticum (pumilum)*, and *E. kotschyanum* is from Asia Minor. Both are low, tidy plants, the latter doing more spreading. *E.* "Jubilee" is a hybrid, larger but very effective. This probably has *E. alpinum* as one of its parents. *E. alpinum* has a lemon form called "Moonlight."

Much taller is *E. capitatum wheeleri*, which flashes out in June with fiery orange, then goes on producing flowers on a stalk which gets longer and longer until the pods ripen and go brown. The whole plant dies at three feet and leaves next year's babies to endure the winter. This biennial is worth growing for its fine color. It may only be a form of *E. asperum*, which has always been yellow when I have grown it from seed.

A mauve wallflower from the Rockies is *Phoenicaulis cheiranthoides* (= *Parrya menziesii*). A really good form of this is worth having. It is possibly short-lived but not usually monocarpic.

If you have ever grown annuals you must be familiar with "ten-week stock." A good rock plant of the same genus is *Matthiola vallesiaca* (may be a subspecies of *M. fruticulosa*). This can be propagated by cuttings and stools out to a chubby mat of violet flowers about six inches high.

In the seedlists you can find other crucifers which are border plants or curiosities: *Barbarea* (variegated leaf but quite coarse); *Biscutella* (a bit tender and probably not worth fussing over); *Hesperis* (dame's rocket, a popular cottage type); *Isatis* (makes a blue dye called woad); *Cardamine* (for damp meadows); *Fibigia* and *Lunaria* (honesty) to make dried flower arrangements using the fruit.

There is one beautiful and almost hardy plant for a container with winter protection—*Morisia monantha*. This has a dark-green, shiny, heavily cut leaves and large yellow flowers sitting on the bun in February and March. *M. monantha* propagates by root cuttings if you pull the plant rather roughly out of its pot leaving bits of root to make new plants. Someone has called it everybody's favorite crucifer, but another candidate is surely *Eunomia oppositifolia*, with blue-green, smooth, rounded leaves on a flat mat. This flowers with the drabas, a very pretty pink. It is sometimes listed (by Farrer and Griffith) as an aethionema, with some confusion about the time of flowering and its hardiness.

Petrocallis pyrenaica can sometimes be found in the seedlists. Get this if you see it, for it is another choice member of the genus, sometimes called a pink draba. Very good too is *Hutchinsia alpina*, which remains a small mat (six inches across after three or four years). The flowers are white and low, the foliage dark green and intricately cut.

The *Brassicas* are crucifers too. We eat the roots of turnip, the stems of kohlrabi, the leaves of cabbage and kale, the buds of broccoli, the flowers of cauliflower, and the seeds of mustard. The bruised leaves of iberis remind you vividly of the English Sunday-dinner smell. The deer go for this aroma and will chomp iberis down to the ground. They eat everything else, too, but iberis is a favorite October appetizer easily as attractive as apples.

The crucifer family is not the most exciting alpine family, but it contains its share of gems and a lot of good bread-and-butter plants that accompany and follow the spring bulbs and keep the garden colorful on and off for half the summer.

Penstemons

IN A COMPETITION amongst groups of plants penstemons would be close to the top of the list. There are many, many species and a wide variety of types, from stately border plants to low mats. Some of the best loved alpines are penstemons. There are not too many contenders for the top of the list of individual penstemons, but several might make the top five for a discriminating gardener. For many years now I have grown at least twenty species of penstemons a year, mostly from seed obtained from the American Penstemon Society. This is more than most people need. I have a severe case of *collectivitis* (abnormal excitement of the possessive instinct), and anyone suffering from this affliction wants to "grow them all." In fact you *can't* grow them all. Some won't grow. Some are the wrong shape, size, or color. Some are unavailable in any seedlist. There is a stream of hybrids that you can't keep up with. And ultimately there is the same cost factor in terms of time, money, space, and energy that undermines all human activity. All these factors obtain with the Genus *Penstemon*.

The flowering period of penstemons is crammed into about five weeks of May and June. This is a period when the rest of the garden is burgeoning and plants that are subtle in their appeal sometimes escape attention. By the end of the season one hopes to have a photographic record with which to analyze the species, note differences, and maybe get all the names straight. My slide file is full of unnamed pents, and part of the reason is a botanical one. Think about primulas. The division into Candelabras, Farinosa, Vernales, etc. types is a real aid in remembering names. The divisions are recognizable, and that is a first step in pinning down the species. Genus *Iris* has a long flowering period starting with the earliest bulbous types and progressing through "pumilas," crested, bearded, siberian, japanese, until well into August the vesper iris appears. I don't say you can identify a species by consulting a calendar, but it does help to have this time spread.

Penstemons seem to resist wholesale classification. Botanists have subdivided the genus into divisions with barbarous names, useful but not easy to grasp. Maybe the plants themselves have something to do with it. Some species are still developing, and species intergrade with each other geographically. This means there are many intermediate forms. All the same there are very distinct species: *P. barbatus* is a tall scarlet plant, while *P. nitidus* is a short robin's-egg-blue beauty, and *P. decumbens* is a mat reminiscent of a gaultheria. There are many ways of handling penstemons in the literature, and it is mildly interesting to compare a few.

The first way, and perhaps the only way acceptable to a botanist—which I hasten to say I am not—is a botanical classification into seven subgenera. Each subgenus has sections, the largest subgenus having ten sections, and many of the sections having subsections. The members of these subsections are the species themselves, though a species may have subspecies, forms, and varieties. In all, the penstemons comprise close to a thousand taxa recognized officially. The intermediate forms blur the definition of these divisions, and the man-made hybrids and selections add to the daunting complexity.

Assume you don't want to embark on a lifetime study of penstemons, how do you start to unravel the mess? The simplest way to classify penstemons is alphabetically! It is what most gardening books do. Obviously only a few of them can be mentioned in any one list. You can find lists in nursery catalogs, rock-garden books, *Hortus*, the *RHS Dictionary*—even Farrer does penstemons alphabetically. Usually the point of the list is to tell you which are worth growing, easy to grow, available to buy, or desirable in some other way. You can learn something about the plants from the descriptions given, but the information is disconnected. Anna Griffith, for example, lists twelve penstemons in her popular *Guide to Alpines*. Half of them are from the section Dasanthera, the shrubby penstemons. Mrs. Griffith's is a good list but not at all a cross section of even the rock-garden penstemons.

Another classification is geographical. If you visit Boulder or Billings on your way into the Rockies, it pays to buy a wildflower book. This will be a catalog of the commonest local flowers, and in it will be a few penstemons. A book like this is to help you identify plants in the wild and will have a classification of its own. Possibly by color, although pents have a way of contradicting color descriptions since moisture and soil often affect their color. A disagreeable aspect of this type of book is that the species are scattered throughout the text, the blue one nowhere near the red one. A rather better way is attempted by Ruth Nelson in her book of Rocky Mountain plants. Here the classification is by type of plant. The sections include mat-forming, large-flowered, tall, clustered, and so on. At least all the penstemons are together, and the descriptions can be compared.

None of these classifications helps you in identifying a plant in your own garden, though. It was a long time before I realized how much more difficult it is for a gardener to identify a plant than for a botanist or a wildflower enthusiast. In the field you are limited to a much narrower range of plants than you are in a garden. Presumably you know exactly where you are; at least you know the country, the state, and whether you are on a mountain or in a forest. In the garden, assuming the plant's origin is a mystery, you may not even know the hemisphere the plant came from. Also the number of plants a ranger needs to remember is finite and small, whereas a rock gardener is trying to retain the names of all the plants in the world in his very finite brain. This may explain why one of our guides at a recent conference in Denver identified a penstemon we had found as "the blue one."

The best and fullest list of names useful to rock gardeners is the one published by the American Penstemon Society in the December 1972 Bulletin. This describes about 120 dwarf penstemons listed by section. Many of us grow taller plants, so even this list has its limitations. Here is a desirable dozen of low penstemons to research: *P.P. confertus, davidsonii, menziesii, eriantherus, fruticosus, hallii, hirsutus* 'Pygmaeus,' *linarioides, pinifolius, procerus, rupicola, nitidus, procumbens.* And a few taller plants: *P.P. digitalis, smallii, haydenii, barrettae, barbatus, arkansanus.*

Each year I take many pictures of penstemons. The colors are mangled by Kodak, the reflection of the sun from the label makes the name illegible on the slide, and if I keep records on scraps of paper I lose them in the laundry. Another year goes by, and I still have dozens of unidentified penstemon slides. The largest all-American genus remains an enigma.

Campanulas

CAMPANULAS ARE LIKE relatives: they come in all shapes and sizes, some of them we love, some of them are a bit boring, a few of them are real pests. Clifford Crook has written a whole book on campanulas. Everybody should own it. Farrer devotes nearly fifty pages to the genus, and it is impossible to find a current book about rock gardening or perennial gardening that fails to mention several species. Here are a few pros and cons.

Against the genus: the limited color range; the sameness of the flower shape; the timing of the flowering period (slightly too late); prolific seed distribution and runners; short life of some species.

For the genus: the color range may be limited, but it is a color—blue—that we all want; and the range of blues goes on all the way from white, cream, and grey through pale blue, deep blue, and into purple. Most of the blues are on the mauvy side, it is true, but there are all kinds of splendid subtleties, from the dove grey of *Campanula cochlearifolia* to the royal purple of *C. glomerata*. The flowers may be all bell shaped, but Nature seems to have rung all the changes on the design from the flared fat bells of *C. medium* to the pinched tubes of *C. zoysii*. And although most campanulas bloom after the main May show and fail to give us the benefit of their rare colors to cool down the display, when they do bloom they seem to give the garden a second wind. Finally, besides the weedy ones, campanulas include some of the most temperamental plants in the rock garden, like *C. piperi* and *C. raineri*. Don't scorn the weedy campanulas; you may need a vigorous plant as part of your plan, for instance in a wild garden or even in a perennial border. Everybody's idea of weed is not the same. As for the short life of some of the species, some of the most beautiful plants are monocarpic, biennial, or annual, and once you know this you can use them accordingly. Either allow them to self-sow or plan to have them for just one season. Here is a rundown of some of the campanulas you are likely to find in seedlists, catalogs, plant sales, and in other people's gardens. I have arranged them by garden use rather than alphabetically, starting with the worst.

Border Campanulas

Very weedy are *C. rapunculoides* and *C. punctata*. Neither plant should be introduced into your garden. *C. punctata* is a very attractive fat-belled white or dusky pink, but it runs and jumps like a thoroughbred. If you have a wild woodland area with a lot of competition you might risk it. *C. alliariifolia* is a border plant that seeds vigorously. It is a pretty creamy white and, if you can control it, well worth growing.

Other border campanulas are: *C. lactiflora*, a large plant with a milky-white shower of bells. Very attractive but hard to get going. There isn't much growth for a couple of years, and the second winter is as bad as the first to get through.

C. pyramidalis is a giant beauty for a large pot near the house. It is perennial but not up to much after the first year. For best results keep it indoors for the winter, grow it in a large pot, and feed it well.

C. latifolia is a handsome plant with rough leaves. A pretty white form comes true from seed.

Everybody knows *C. persicifolia*. There are a number of clones not much better than the species. These cost a lot and do not always establish well. The biggest fault with *C. persicifolia* is its tendency to make a good big mat of leaves and then not send up many flower stalks. Frequent division seems to help keep healthy plants. A plant called *C. nitida* or *C. planiflora* is supposed to be a dwarf form of *C. persicifolia*, but they are very dissimilar, and seed does not come true.

C. thyrsoides is the nearly yellow campanula, the same color as "yellow" gentians. Worth growing, but it is not a ravishing plant.

C. rigidipila and *C. sarmatica* are also large. Perhaps the most satisfactory border campanula is *C. glomerata*, especially if you get a good deep color. There is a clone of this called "Joan Elliot" which is earlier and a deeper color than the average seedling. There are forms of *C. glomerata* called *nana* which are still pretty big and revert to regular size when they start self-sowing in the garden.

Biennial, Monocarpic, & Annual Campanulas

C. medium is the familiar Canterbury bells with nice fat flowers. Sometimes you get a cup-and-saucer form, which some people don't like. *C. speciosa* is similar but shorter.

There are a number of biennial campanulas from the Balkans,

including *C. orphanidea, C. lyrata,* and *C. rupestris.* These have
attractive grey leaves and need at least a foot of spreading room
to display their charms. *C. lyrata* self-sows for me. It looks
good sprawling on a flat scree or molding itself along a rock.
Small plants flat on the ground are *C. sartori* and *C. calamen-
thifolia.* These have substantial small bells. They also self-sow,
but the first plants you grow from seed seem to be the heartiest.

   C. barbata is a foot high, and both blue and white forms are
very pretty. The bell is hairy, more like the moustache of a
youth than a real beard.

   C. carpatica is a vigorous rock plant with large open bells
which comes in many strains and forms (e.g., *C. turbinata*). *C.
cochleariifolia* has charming cheeky bells. One form of this is
called "Miranda," and I cannot get it established. Let it run
around wherever it wants to go. It will die out quickly if it runs
out of lebensraum. *C. rotundifolia* is another very vigorous plant
with many forms and a pageful of synonyms. It seems to grow
all over the northern hemisphere, and one ought to try seed
from several sources to get the benefit of the extensive variation.

   C. kemmulariae has purplish bells and grows strongly without
seeding around. *C. portenschlagiana* and *C. poscharskiana* are both
strong growers.

   Good rock plants include *C. aucheri.* My plants have a white
base. *C. betulaefolia* has lovely pink buds and opens white. *C.
garganica* and its relatives *C. fenestrellata* and *C. elatines* are reliable in many people's gardens. *C. tommasiniana* too is a good
plant which, like the others, forms mats which are more or less
permanent. *C. waldsteiniana* is daintier and forms a tuft like a
taller *cochleariifolia. C. pilosa (= C. dasyantha)* is a fairly easy
plant of which one form comes from Japan.

   The really difficult campanulas are sometimes available in
seedlists and catalogs. Get hold of them whenever you can; you
may have instant success and be the envy of the chapter. Look
for *C. cenisia, C. excisa, C. morettiana, C. piperi, C. zoysii,* and
C. raineri. These are not just difficult, they are really beautiful
plants and worth a shot if you have a sunny scree. I have flowered a few of them occasionally as have a number of people,
but the only one that stays around for any length of time is *C.*

raineri. Seed of this one is usually a hybrid with *C. carpatica*, so beware bragging until you are certain you really have the true plant.

Most of the alpine campanulas need well-drained soil, even scree, and they mostly tolerate light shade. As far as the genus *Campanula* is concerned I have only scratched the surface, and you should try any others from seed that come your way. Remember those obnoxious relatives, though, and check out the name if you can before you let a campanula loose in the garden.

Summer Bulbs

DOES THE PHRASE "summer bulbs" bring to mind hybrid lilies, dinner-plate dahlias, cannas, and fat gladioli? There are bulbs, corms, and tubers that bloom in the summer and fit gracefully into a rock garden. Some of them need a little bit of care, but nothing quite as depressing as handling those prolific tubers that dahlias manufacture by the basketful. A number of bulbs are easy in the sense that we can leave them in the garden all year, and so the question becomes one of hitting a convenient spot for them. Many oxalis are rather weedy (that is, their bulbs multiply at a phenomenal rate), and nearly all of them have leaves reminiscent of that little yellow horror that engulfs our gardens in July and persists until hard frost wipes out the remnants. *Oxalis adenophylla* is a gem with pleated leaves and beautiful pink flowers. It survives Massachusetts winters unprotected and is very well behaved. It also looks right in a rock garden. You may have to discipline your emotional response in order to accept its right to belong. *O. adenophylla* is from Chile and Argentina. From South Africa comes *O. inops*, a.k.a. *O. depressa*, having a good deep pink, a more solid color than the previous. You should take some of it indoors for the winter and leave some outside, as it sometimes comes through. *O. lobata*, also from South America, is a treasure with beautiful yellow flowers, so put it where the weed isn't or you won't like it. It ought to be as hardy as *O. adenophylla*, but I still lose it outside. There are a number of other oxalis readily available, but beware of some of the woodlanders. If you can grow them at all they will probably take over great sheets of ground. Of course that may be exactly what you want.

There are two or three bulbs that are right nowhere but are so beautiful that it is worth trying to find a good place for them. *Hymenocallis caroliniana (syn. occidentalis)* is nearly hardy and probably would be in the Connecticut banana belt. This is an "Ismene" from Georgia. *Galtonia candicans* is just as hard to place and nearly hardy (I had survivors for two winters). Both are out of place in a perennial bed and much too large for a rock garden, but you might find a place for a couple of specimen plants at the edge of the woodland, or try the hymenocallis in a bog. *Lycoris squamigera* is a fully hardy bulb which looks quite good with larger rock plants. It needs room, as colchicums do, for the thick straplike leaves that occupy space in spring and die back before the flower stalk rises in August. They look okay hugging the skirts of a conifer or a shrub that provides background material for a rock bed. Other semihardy bulbs are from the genera *Zephyranthes* and *Habranthus*. Often you can get *Z. candida, Z. citrina,* and *Z. rosea* as well as *H. robustus*. Sonia Lowzow insists these are hardy in her cold Arizona garden. They probably need very good drainage to survive the winters here, and I have not managed to keep them outside so far. I usually take them inside after the leaves have started to brown but before a really hard frost. I replant them in pots ready for next spring and put them under the bench of a cold but not frozen greenhouse. Mice like to gnaw the bulbs' outer layer, so you have to watch for marauders. I long to grow the species gladioli, *Gladiolus byzantinus* for instance, but bulbs are never offered, and the seeds I have sown have yet not developed into flowering-size bulbs. Has anyone out there succeeded, and are any of them New England hardy?

Alliums, too, are summer bulbs, but nearly all are hardy and qualify as rock-garden plants not included in this group.

Gardening in the Woods

WHAT DO YOU do with a woodlot? The meadow can be tamed. You dig out the sod, pile it up to make the next raised bed, improve the soil, and in the process remove as many small and middle-sized-rocks as you can. If you can bring the large ones to the surface they can be used as decoration or standing stations, otherwise they remain below the surface to haunt you when you plant out. A meadow has so many possibilities, and at worst you can keep mowing it until grass predominates. Actually we have so many Quaker ladies *(Houstonia caerulea)* that mowing is delayed until they have flowered. A sea of Quaker ladies is infinitely preferable to coarse grass. *Phlox subulata* seeds itself over yards of "lawn," so that is also mowed around until the flowers have gone.

But the woodland represents a great investment in time and labor. Using a chain saw is not my idea of fun, and it costs money to remove trees. Once you have started neatening the border country between meadow and wood, a whole new world of gardening opens up. New plants, new methods, a new aesthetic. Building a fake cliff in the middle of the lawn deceives nobody into thinking it is a real mountain, for in an open garden artifice is taken for granted. But if you invade woodland, the trees, or most of them, will remain, and the ambience is definitely that of the edge of a New England forest. One possibility is to make a garden in the wood, that is, a collection of beds. Another is to add a few alien plants to the existing vegetation, hoping to transform the picture for a brief period in spring. This could be done with English bluebells or cowslips. All that is needed then is to tidy up the trash. There are all stages intermediate between these points of view. You could even plant a forest and call it an arboretum, where trees are the main interest, but this requires half a lifetime or a fortune or both. Even in the extreme case of making a garden in the forest there will be a kind of built-in naturalness that you won't want to fight except to provide paths for access. The planting will be plants that look right without trying and that want to grow there—woodlanders, not high alpines. If you mistakenly plant a sun lover in the woods it will tell you your taste is at fault by sulking and then dying.

HOUSTONIA CAERULEA, *Quaker Ladies or Bluets, prefers sun.*

Starting a woodland garden is easier in some ways and harder in others than starting a rock garden. The scale is different; more ground has to be covered to make an effect. A tiny scree can hold a hundred jewels with year-round interest, but a patch of woodland the same size will hold a couple of species which will have very little impact at high season and be completely invisible most of the year. In other words it is pointless to go into the woods and plant one primrose.

Once you have realized the magnitude of the area needed to gain some kind of effect, it will occur to you that some planning is desirable. You have to get rid of enough trees, usually two or three times as many as you first anticipate, to get the dappled shade—not deep shade—that will be congenial to most plants. Select a few trees, the best shaped, the least weedy, to keep. Then hire somebody to cut down the unwanted trees if you are the least bit squeamish about cutting them down yourself, and unless you want to spend fall, winter, and part of spring working endlessly with a chain saw and a tractor. It may take several seasons before you are satisfied that there is enough light to grow the plants you want. However destructive you are, the remaining trees will try to fill the airspace with their own leafage when the competition has gone, and you may have to keep hacking away at the native scrub a third year. Be very firm about getting rid of diseased trees and twisted saplings. The point is, you will forget in two days the trees that were blemished and rejoice in the newly introduced light and the airy feeling that only a clearing in a wood can give.

When you are ready to plant, the first thing you think of may be rhododendrons. Remember, the small-leafed species usually want plenty of sunlight, and so do azaleas, so it isn't necessary to overstuff your space with these. Many rhododendrons do need protection from full sun that dappled shade provides, and it is very enjoyable to plant small specimens of species rhododendrons and watch the less-hardy ones succumb to winter hardships and to discover the ones that will grow into flowering size for you. Waiting for rhododendrons to bloom is midway between the almost instant gratification of perennials and the long-term wait for a tree to mature.

SHORTIA GALACIFOLIA, *woodland plant from the
Southern Appalachians.*

But it is the flowers of the forest that are really interesting as
far as I am concerned. The trilliums, tricyrtis, shortias, woodland phlox and silenes, the gingers and their relatives, the
hepaticas and the primulas that combine to make spring in a
woodland garden such a joy.

Before you plant in the woods you have to prepare the ground.
First consider the problem of getting rid of the grass, the solidago and aster, and the ferns that eked out their lives under
the almost unbroken panoply formed by the tops of the spindly
trees that you started with. There are three ways possible: kill
chemically, kill by suppression, or dig up. Digging up has the
disadvantages of being hard work, and you lose precious soil
to the compost heap. It is astonishing how little real soil there
is under the trees—mostly roots, rocks, and air. If you suppress
there are several possible methods: tin roofing, old carpets,
newspapers, plastic, old hay bales—almost anything with square
yardage that will lie flat either solo or with the help of rocks

and logs. Nothing I have tried is pretty. Newspapers are good because the worms eat them and improve what soil there is; their disadvantage is their tendency to blow about when the wind gets between the sheets, no matter how you weight them down. I have used professional journals which I held on to after retiring until I realized I was hooked on gardening and would never read the accumulated wisdom of the last decade. There are new products in the garden centers made of water-permeable plastic which suppress pretty well but have to be paid for. Chemicals are also possible, but since I am deathly afraid of their effects on me as well as on that part of the environment not scheduled for destruction, I tend to delay and finally avoid using them. You may feel more carefree about these Agent Orange substitutes. Taking everything into consideration preparation of woods for gardening will take about a year of lead time. A gradual approach is also possible, but the work has to be done whether in dribs and drabs or all at once. Plenty of ex-students, nephews, and Girl Scouts cut down the time, too.

When the ground is ready to start planting, be as generous in your use of planting materials as you can afford to be. If it is primulas you will plant, grow them from seed in quantity; if it is eastern wildflowers, there are plenty of nurseries that sell them. Avoid nurseries that desecrate the environment by digging up thousands of wildflowers each year to send by mail to customers unwilling to admit complicity in the vandalism.

Start with relatively easy plants even if you can afford and are impatient to have expensive, difficult ones. The first year you are virtually certain to be disappointed; for one thing, you are invading the home territory of several wild animals. Deer will eat the tops of trilliums, and moles will tunnel through any disturbed or imported soil. The first planting I did of trilliums, orchids, uvullaria, and asarums ended up two years later with just three trilliums and, of course, the local weeds. You can poison and kill if you feel inclined, but it ends up better value to be resigned to some losses and make the takeover gradual. Eventually you may want an electric fence to guard your treasures. My advice is to restrain your enthusiasm for buying everything in sight until such time as you have worked out your attitude towards and strategy against animals.

Now for a short list of plants that will give great pleasure for a brief time and some pleasure all the time. Most of them have a brief flowering period but interesting, even exquisite, foliage that creates a tapestry of greens in the woodland and opens your eyes to foliage plants in other situations.

The woodland garden is neither like a perennial border nor a rock garden in the choice and arrangement of plants, and it may be best to list plants by their growth habits. Nearly every woodland plant has been described as a "ground cover" by somebody or other, and there are a number of them which are vigorous enough to cover large areas quickly given the right conditions. Many of them are best bought as established plants in containers or through the mails, bare-root. Bare-root plants can be tricky to establish, and it is worthwhile trying out a few patches in different locations as well as trying to get some started in a pot before actually planting out. The trouble with this latter method is the size of the roots—usually too long for your largest available pot. However if you get bits and pieces which seem expendable among the massive tangle of the main buy, don't discard them; they may be the only plants that get established. Seed is not usually worth the trouble or the wait when the local wildflowers are so easy to obtain otherwise.

Asarums. The gingers are grown for their beautiful leathery leaves. There are plenty of species or subspecies in the southeast; you may get them under the genus name *Hexastylis. A. canadense* has rather dull leaves which will set off the glossier, silver-streaked leaves of *A. hartwegii.* Other names to look for are *A. virginicum* and a western ginger, *A. caudatum.* There is more fun in collecting interesting forms than names. The European *A. europaeum* is also glossy and can be beautifully marked. Nobody can tell at a glance which species you have. The flowers of all these plants are attractive brown cups with flared rims, but they're impossible to see unless you get on your hands and knees to lift the leaves. You might pot one in flower and put it on the dining table, where it will excite admiration from anybody who loves architecture and sculpture.

With the same sumptuous effect are two plants having the

PHLOX DIVARICATA 'FULLER'S WHITE': *Canadian phlox,*
usually misty blue, has white and mauve forms.

added virtue of visible flowers. *Galax aphylla* has round leathery leaves with airy stalks of starry flowers. The flowers don't last long, but a large group can be very effective. *Shortia galacifolia* has similar leaves, as its name implies, but the flowers are exquisite white-frilled bells even shorter-lived than galax. Shortia is fairly difficult to establish; buy it in containers even though it will be expensive if you buy enough to cover a large area. The new leaves in spring unfold with all kinds of pinkish tinges which makes them look vulnerable and precious. Possibly the loveliest of American woodlanders. There is a Japanese cousin, *Shortia soldanelloides*, more delicate, more pink, and more difficult.

Some ground covers give a flashier display of color, especially the phlox. *P. divaricata* is the classic with good blue (tinge of mauve) flowers. There is also a white form which shows up well in shady areas. These stand about a foot and a half tall and have leaves smoother than the moss pink and not so coarse as the border phlox. They grow perfectly well in sun, too. A plant from south Georgia called 'Chattahoochee' is probably a form of *divaricata* which has more intense color including a reddish eye, and is not so vigorous. *Phlox stolonifera*, too, doesn't mind shade. This has its mat flat on the ground and needs to be clear of competition until established but takes care of itself easily afterwards. There are many color forms; if you mix them they will cancel each other out. 'Irridescens' is a mix of blue and white but glows, 'Pink Ridge' is a not very clean pink, and there are almost-purples and a good white—no real blues. Other good phlox include *P. pilosa*, *P. ovata*, and hybrids such as *P. X procumbens*. One is always torn between collecting as many species and forms as possible and creating a coherent picture. In a woodland garden it may be better to de-emphasize the collector's instinct and humor the landscaper.

There are other ground covers, such as *Pulmonaria saccharata*, of the mottled leaves and flowers, that go from almost-pink to almost-blue. *P. montana* is a nice pink, and *P. angustifolia* a good blue. Close in general effect is *Symphytum grandiflorum*, with pale-yellow flowers, which colonizes steadily and flowers a little later than the pulmonarias. *Iris cristata* will cover a square yard

IRIS CRISTATA, *at home at the edge of the woodland.*

in a couple of years. The white form seems to be even more vigorous than the blue of the species, and there are several selected forms with deeper color or more petite flowers.

Below the ground covers are creeping plants that roam amongst their neighbors or form nice low patches if you can keep their neighbors away from them. Very special is *Linnaea borealis*, which has its two-inch-high flower pairs growing from wiry stolons. This is very easy to uproot carelessly, so an established patch is to be treasured. *Epigaea repens* is also difficult to get going but worth a few tries. *Claytonia virginica* and various montias are a little easier but lack the elegance of trailing arbutus or twinflower. If you can handle a real wanderer that may become a pest you could plant *Oxalis oregana* or some other woodland oxalis. An easier easterner is *Mitchella repens*; you may have to search for the flowers, but the berries are bright in fall.

Above the ground covers are larger plants which would not be out of place in a border. Foxgloves and bleeding heart, for instance. *Dicentra eximia* forms mounds of succulent divided leaves with pink flowers well above the leaves. In a woodland setting it is an eye-catcher. The white form is equally attractive. Both dicentras are pests in the border or rock garden but precious in the woods. *Dicentra spectabilis* is prettier but not as showy or vigorous, and its white form is a gem. *D. cucullaria* is very flimsy looking but looks after itself quite well. It forms tubers that can be dug up and spread around after the plant dies down quite early in the summer. There is a peach-colored form found in Pennsylvania, the normal color being a pure white.

A group of silenes and members of the Saxifrage family are also great plants for this showy middle-sized tier of the woodland garden. *Silene wherryi* and *S. virginica*, the first pink and the second a startling red, are both hardy quite far north. *Tiarella wherryi* has a flower which is far from showy, but the leaves can be marked with deep maroon patches. Tellimas and mitellas are there for the collectors, looking more like inferior heucheras unless your interest changes "like" to "love." *Saxifraga virginiensis* and *S. pennsylvanica*, the one short, the other a giant three-footer, are useful for adding solid looking leaves and the promise of flowers. *Tricyrtis* species are also at this very visible height

MITCHELLA REPENS. *The partridgeberry is a good ground cover for shade.*

and have a clumpy look when established, but the flowers themselves are not showy except at close range. The easiest is *T. hirta* with its spotted purple flowers. *T. flava* and *T. macrantha* are yellow, luscious but not gaudy. A collection of these Asian plants is tempting.

The greatest joys of the woodland garden are the short-lived flowers of early spring: trilliums, hepaticas, ladyslippers, anemones, anemonellas, jeffersonias, sanguinarias, uvullarias, and iris. These can be dotted around or massed. You can "collect" with equanimity: the more forms and species, the more pleasure. Fifteen species of trillium will look like each other after the flowers are gone but are full of individuality in flower, and leaves of the double bloodroot look just like the single. *Jeffersonia dubia* has distinctive leaves, so does *J. diphylla*, and nobody will object to either a specimen or a carpet of either one. *J. dubia* has variable color, but the deep mauve of the best forms is almost unique in the garden, and its habit of self-sowing is charming and valuable.

If yours is a weekend garden there may be years when you completely miss seeing *Sanguinaria canadensis* and *Jeffersonia diphylla*, because their bloom time is so short. Get hold of the double form of bloodroot, it lasts longer and is a spectacular flower. So is the double form of *Trillium grandiflorum*. The white form of *Trillium erectum* is off-white and squinnier than the common "purple" kind. The plants called *T. luteum* and *T. chloropetalum* have nice mottled leaves and flowers that look as though they should open some more but never do. There is some disarray where names of trilliums are concerned, but all types are worth growing, although if you collect you get some disappointing specimens. Later on the arisaemas start: the common Jack-in-the-pulpit (*Arisaema triphyllum*) will probably be a "pest" in your woodland. It will look right wherever you leave it and only needs to be restrained from invading expensive introductions. There are a number of spectacular Asian jacks that are hard to get but give an aristocratic air to an open space. *A. sikokianum* is a beauty, and so are several others. These are definitely plants to collect next time you visit a Tokyo nursery.

Taller than the display-making plants are the towering specimen plants. It will be very much a matter of taste which to grow. A good choice might be one of the cimicifugas. *Cimicifuga racemosa* is five feet tall with plumes in summer. Others flower at different times. You might find a place for the monster leaves of a *Rodgersia*, especially if you have a damp spot. The larger Solomon's seals also make an interesting break in the vegetation level. They wander around, and you have to accept their current position permissively. *Polygonatum commutatum* is the big one, and there are others of varying heights that fit into all the categories except the creepers. The smallest are *P. falcatum* and even smaller *P. humile*, which is only about six inches high.

Finally the primroses look well and grow well in woodland conditions. The word "primrose" usually denotes *Primula vul-*

TIARELLA WHERRYI, *a foamflower without stolons.*

garis, but it loosely covers all members of the Vernales section of the genus *Primula*: this would include *P. veris, P. elatior, P. juliae, P. amoena,* as well as a host of species and subspecies with names like *P. uralensis, P. carpathica, P. columnae,* etc., which turn out to be forms of the others. In addition to the species primulas are the forms and hybrids, especially two groups the 'Juliana' hybrids, which always have some *P. juliae* ancestry, and the polyanthus group. These latter are mostly hybrids of *P. vulgaris* and *P. veris.* Here tastes differ widely. Some people spend their lives breeding large-flowered polyanthus with every color of the rainbow; others regard them as ostentatious and only fit for bedding outside a savings bank. Some gardeners restrict themselves to *vulgaris* forms, with one flower on a stem, or to *juliana* forms, with their characteristic creeping habit. There is also the question of mixing colors or separating them into groups. I like primroses of all kinds in all ways. A large group of mixed brightly colored polyanthus will not look natural in a wood, but who cares? It is for such a short period of time that the forest blazes, and you can keep them away from the delicate hepaticas and anemones if you are hung up on purity.

A woodland garden is very leavable in the summer, especially if you have mulched the ground with shredded leaves or buckwheat hulls. When you have an established garden in the wood you can plant orchids—*Orchis spectabilis, Cypripedium reginae*—and some of the rarer lilies near the edges: *Lilium grayi,* and how about trying *Nomocharis saluenensis?* Your ultimate triumph will be to get a stand of *Meconopsis betonicifolia* going. Seed is easy to obtain and not so easy to raise, but it can be done. Until you have somewhere to put the plants, obviously, there is no point in trying.

Late Bloomers

D o you grow *Anemone 'Japonica'?* These beautiful plants are probably hybrids of *A. hupehensis* and are really border plants. Certainly not suitable for an area where they might jostle small buns and mats. They provide a flash of glory when the garden is almost colorless, and they act as ground cover for a good part of the year. This exposes their main fault, which is occupying space for so long and always under the threat of an early hard freeze which could render the long wait futile. If you can live with this disadvantage and accept the bad with the good, you might be interested in other plants with the same characteristics. Familiar examples are the colchicums. Give them lots of room to make their massive leaves in spring. Some people complain about the leaves, but they are not unattractive, just *big*, so make allowances and find space for *Colchicum speciosum* and its forms. Later the autumn crocuses appear, and several of these are worth growing. *Crocus speciosus* has some excellent forms, and *C. sativus* is a gem.

There are a number of composites which bloom in October too and would bloom into November some years. *Serratula seaonei* is a quaint plant with many purple flowers and attractive leaves, about six inches high. Seed appears in the seed exchanges, but the name is sometimes corrupted to *S. shawii.* The genus *Heterotheca* contains some late-blooming yellow daisies. *H. pinifolia* has very narrow leaves and asterlike flowers. *H. gossypina* has greyish leaves with almost no stalk that curl in an attractive way. *H. mariana* has smoother, reddish leaves. All these plants can be obtained from WeDu Nursery. Some aconitums bloom very late too. *Aconitum fischeri* can have flowers after the middle of October.

We enjoy the unplanned late bloomers as a bonus: the leftover campanulas and the premature primulas, not to mention annuals which are reluctant to call it a day. How about planning for a late show? Incidentally *Ipomopsis aggregata* is a very late annual which I have had self-sow. The seedlings don't seem to appear until July or August, and the flowering begins at the end of the summer. Perhaps the most welcome end-of-the-season display comes from *Kniphofia galpinii* with soft orange spikes out of a grassy clump of foliage. The seed is sometimes found in the seedlists.

A Favorite Tree

D O YOU HAVE a favorite plant in your garden? Really favorite? Everybody has a collection of favorites but usually wouldn't want to choose just one of them to be *it*, partly because our criteria change from one plant to the next. This one is a favorite because it is a fabulous blue, this one because it is especially rare, and this one because it is just very happy growing right where it is and looks heartwarmingly healthy. I often wonder how people who grow only hemerocallis or bearded iris manage to handle their blinders where other genera are concerned.

There is a plant in our garden which qualifies as favorite especially when visitors arrive. Every tour takes it in, and it always merits a five-minute huddle as its history and qualities are rehashed once again.

And it isn't even my plant.

It is a weeping Japanese larch. An eight-foot-high fountain of larchy branches which wash over onto the lawn in a yard-wide skirt. In spring the new leaves are fresh and soft as a two-year-old baby's hair; in summer they are green and have roughened up to velvet. Fall brings on a change to orange which comes ostentatiously after the maples have shed their magnificence. The larch is one of the few deciduous conifers (another is Genus *Taxodium*); after a week and a couple of gales it is left with an intricate framework of branches rather like a wire dress form for an eighteenth-century fat lady.

While the tree has its needles, it looks like a wig, a rather tacky shoulder-length undisguised wig that could have been used in a TV drama about one of the Beatles. As this year's bonus, a robin made its nest in the center at head height and enhanced the illusion of hair falling around a mysterious face. We saw the eggs in there, but the nest was abandoned before hatching after a marauder also discovered the nest in July.

Liking this plant is easy. It is a curiosity, it is graceful, it is variable through the year ("provides interest," as they say), and it is non-hostile, unlike the spruces and junipers which can pierce the skin with their hearty needles. It is also relatively rare and not so easy to propagate, and very few nurseries carry it. It displays an element of the gardener himself. Because of its growth habit you have to do something with it—support it or fail to support it. Whatever the gardener does has an effect. Take a leader another foot higher and you change a turtle into a parasol. The tree reflects the gardener's attitude and waits for the gardener's whimsy to determine its posture and habit.

Our larch reflects N.'s attitude, since it's his plant. Alas. But I don't really want it myself. It's very nice to have something one can be objective about without the customary possessiveness. It means I can't touch it, either to stake it or to prune it, but then I don't enjoy either of these occupations. It also means any criticism must be made obliquely and diplomatically if it is to be effective. And this poses a problem, as N.'s idea of any kind of construction work is even more ramshackle than mine. This explains the hideous piece of waterpipe that supports the larch with an angle joint remaining on it obviously designed to carry water round a bend, and it accounts for the armature of chicken wire meant to hold the skirt in place and looking forlornly ineffectual in the cruel winter light. Small aptitude for building is also behind the miscellaneous bits of string, relics of other horticultural endeavors, that happened to be in a pocket when something needed to be tied up. But once spring arrives, all this vanishes, and the tree has enough dignity to camouflage these trivial blemishes.

Yes, it is easy to like, but to have as a favorite? There is really nothing about our larch's essence that I admire at all, First, it is non-flowering, which ought to rule it out automatically. Next, it is woody. I am not drawn to long-lived woody objects. I prefer herbaceous short-lived plants and alpines with tight buns and mats. I fear that air of permanence which proclaims, "I am here forever. You will be dead first." And above all I dislike the feeling that it will grow too large for me to ever move again. It offends my need to have flexibility, a garden I can change my mind about and rearrange if I want to.

And then, the thing isn't an alpine at all. *Larix leptolepis* is a tree that grows up to a hundred feet in its native Japan. But worst of all it is a sort of freak, a disadvantaged tree that is genetically incapable of keeping its branches upright unaided and is so recalcitrant that it has to be grafted to another larch to be propagated at all. I spend my time trying to make real, red-blooded alpines grow from mountain-fresh seed—the genuine article. And if for some ridiculous ideological reason they refuse to grow, out they go. Yet here is this wimp which we fondly describe as the leader in the Retreat from Moscow, weeping its way into the Top Ten. And then getting the Emmy.

How on earth is taste formed? It seems you can come to plants with all kinds of prejudices and opinions, but they melt away like April snow when the right example shows up. Beware of generalizations and prejudices; it may turn out you could like orchids! Or daylilies! If the right one should come along.

What's Wrong with Growing Annuals?

I KEEP COMING back to this subject with slight feelings of guilt and a chip on my shoulder. Let's answer the question first and get the bad stuff out of the way. Face it: there is plenty wrong.

1.) *Public opinion*. It is hard to buck the consensus when it includes just about every rock-garden writer who ever set pen to paper. There is either a snide dismissal of annuals or a conspiracy of silence; in either case a complete blackout of information.

2.) *Banality*. If you go to a nursery that sells annuals you find the same six or seven market packs year after year. If you go to a specialist nurseyman who "really knows his plants" you might find salpiglossis or *Salvia farinacea* amongst the marigolds and petunias. You might increase your choice to about twenty kinds.

3.) *Availability*. If you grow your own annuals from seed you get to peruse all the catalogs: Thomson and Morgan, Park's, Burpee's, Di Georgio's, etc. Suddenly your choice has expanded enormously, but you will go through all the lists in four or five years, and you may soon write these off as commonplace too. Sooner or later you have to find other sources.

4.) *Unsuitability*. It's true that no high alpines are annuals. It is also true that petunias look ridiculous next to saxifrages. You have to be discerning about choice of material and about placement if you want to grow annuals in a rock garden.

5.) *Nuisance value*. First, there is the fact that annuals really can grow large during the season. They need plenty of space and a sharp lookout for their effect on near neighbors. Second, they may self-sow. If you don't want them back you have the bother of weeding out the seedlings. If you do want them back you have to decide what is a weed or end up scratching out all the baby annuals. Also you have to leave space for them to develop.

6.) *Trouble*. If annuals don't self-sow you have to raise new plants each year. If you want to prolong their season you have to dead-head. If their season is short you have to fill in. You are almost obliged to collect seed, especially of new introductions. Annuals often need better conditions than rock plants: more watering, more feeding.

7.) *Gaudiness*. You don't like gaudy? Why are you gardening?

None of these is an adequate reason for not growing annuals. I now mention a few of the positive aspects.

1.) *Knowledge*. There is a great range of neglected plants that can be tried. Search for them in the American Rock Garden Society seedlist and any of the other non-commercial seedlists. Don't waste time on the highly developed strains of common annuals unless you really want them—there are so many other possibilities. Of course your interest may be breeding new strains, in which case you might be thinking commercial thoughts.

2.) *Length of season*. Actually I don't dead-head or even cut flowers to put in vases. I don't value long life too highly, and I like to see the passage of the seasons, so I am not unduly concerned when an annual expires after blooming. But you can expect a much longer flowering period for annuals than for most perennial plants.

3.) *Color*. I like color in the garden, and you can get color from annuals from May through November. Annuals are not the first flowers to bloom in the spring, but some annuals are usually the last to be cut down by hard frost. *Aster bigelovii* was still blooming in mid-November this year.

4.) *Challenge*. Well, there are several. You have to find annuals, grow them from seed, and find a place for them in your garden. One good place I have found for annuals is the patio garden, which has the advantages of being visible from the kitchen, being in full sun, and not containing other plants which cannot fend for themselves.

Now a word about raising annuals. You can sow them as you would alpines in three-inch pots in some kind of soilless mixture. Sow them a little later in the year. April is not too late, March if you know they are hardy. The seeds germinate rapidly and often profusely, so thin sowing is *de rigueur*. Transplant into individual pots before the roots get into a hopeless tangle. Some people like flats, but I never want a lot of one kind of plant, so a flat seems excessive. Don't plant them out in the garden until they are pretty sturdy. You may want to wait until a patch of bulbs has stopped flowering and plant nearby, but keep the dying bulb foliage from obliterating the seedlings. Later you will want to temper your care of the annuals by remembering that just under the surface of the soil is a bulb which may not like too much water or large doses of 10–10–10. Anyway, I am not going to find a place for your annuals, and I am certainly not going to recommend them as a ground cover over species tulips. You can solve those problems yourself. A few annuals, such as poppies, are sometimes recommended to be sown where they are to grow. The theory is that they are difficult to transplant. I have never had trouble transplanting, and I have never succeeded in growing plants in situ— except carrots and beans.

Now for a short list of annuals and a few biennials I have grown recently; some of them can be found in the glossies, but most are not in commerce.

Abronia latifolia. Sand verbena is flat, sprawling, fleshy. Needs good drainage.

Adonis aestivalis. Germination unreliable. Flowers a good unusual dark red but not very large. Eight inches tall. You can find this in catalogs.

Androsace albana. Biennial. Looks good with any alpines.

Antirrhinum braun-blanquettii. Probably a perennial but rushes to flower in midsummer. Yellow snapdragons, but different leaves from the usual. What a name!

Aster bigelovii. A great plant from Arizona. Large woody bush covered with lilac flowers. Some plants gave up the ghost in August, some bloomed until November.

Aubrieta pinardii. Two different botanists said this was not an aubrieta. Interesting but not pretty.

Calandrinia grandiflora. Tender perennial like a large talinum. Showy, but bloomed a bit too close to the first frost for comfort.

Calceolaria mexicana. Self-sows well, and it is always admired when it blooms in August. Bright yellow flowers.

Campanula lyrata. Biennial. Pretty Greek. Grey leaves. Self-sows.

Centaurium erythraea. Names of this genus are very confused. This one acts like an annual. Worth having, though not as elegant as *C. scilloides*, which is perennial. A deep-pink relative of the gentians.

Chaenorrhinum origanifolium and *C. glareosum* are neat little purple relatives of linaria. If Farrer is correct the second is a splendid high-alpine mat, but the name came attached to a plant slightly taller than *C. origanifolium*. Don't bother to grow *C. minus*, which is dim and weedy.

Collinsia grandiflora. Flashy medium-sized blue and cream from the West.

Commelina caerulea. A bright-blue tradescantia-type flower. Too much like a local weed for some people. *C. dianthifolia* from Arizona is neater, and I am hoping this one will be perennial.

Crepis rubra. A pink hawkweed. A favorite, but it refuses to self-sow. I collect the seed every year. Color of spun candy.

Dimorphotheca aurantiaca. Get this anywhere. Germination may be poor. Beautiful colors. Coffee daisies—orange, too.

Dorotheanthus hallii. A mesem that blooms early and dies quickly. Give it scree. Ignore the sniffs of visitors from southern California, who are likely to be prejudiced against this large family of beautiful plants.

Dyssodia filifolium. Another Dahlborg daisy.

Emilia flammea. Rather gawky but a good color. This is a red "hawkweed." Seed available commercially.

Eschscholtzia caespitosa. Plant this small yellow poppy with the alpines. Not pushy and self-sows attractively.

Eucharidium breweri. Strange torn-up flowers. A pink clarkia.

Gilia capitata. Powder-blue heads, quietly charming.

Gilia aggregata. Sometimes called ipomopsis. Tall, scarlet bugles. Plant a group together. This plant self-sows, but the seedlings don't appear until July. Don't scratch.

Glaucium flavum. A good horned poppy; that means the seed pod is thin, very long, and curved. Nice peachy color.

Iberis amara is white, *Iberis umbellata* is purple. Both rather alike otherwise in effect. *I. amara* is the one that has been improved by breeders.

Lactuca perennis. Lovely blue relative of lettuce. Self-sows moderately.

Legousia specularis. Said to be weedy. Not spectacular blue.

Lupinus texensis. Very good low lupin. It is not better than the best alpine lupins, but it's a beautiful plant. Needs eighteen inches across at least. Any other lupins are worth trying, but most of them are fairly difficult and may give up the ghost without warning or obvious cause.

LychnisX kubotae. There are a number of similar lychnis species, I think of them as from Japan, but I'm not certain. They may be perennial when happy, or biennial, but for me they seem to be annual. Good orangey-scarlet colors on rangy plants. *L. wilfordii* and *L. miqueliana* are other names to look for.

Mesembryanthemum criniflorum. Neon colors in a "daisy" plant with succulent leaves. The "petals" are stamens. Grow in a hot dry place, and don't show your California friends. There are other mesems listed in Park's, etc.

Mimulus cardinalis. Good scarlet color but rather leafy. There are other *Mimulus* species with collectors' numbers. For me they are mostly annual. All of them are worth growing, and the low ones fit quite well into a rock garden on the shady side, even a bog.

Nemophila maculata and *N. menziesii.* The latter is "baby blue-eyes" and easy to find. The first is less bright but has interesting markings on the flowers. It peters out rather early in the season, so you will want to have something else waiting in the wings as a stand-in.

Nigella damascena and *N. hispanica* are supposed to be different plants but look the same to me. Very attractive blue love-in-a-mist with seed pods just as pretty as the flowers. They are rather exuberant and can travel long distances via the compost heap. Another less available *Nigella* came from the Canterbury, New Zealand seedlist as *N. sp.* and is only six inches tall and a dusky pink. I collected seed but only had a couple of plants the second season.

Omphalodes linifolia. This comes with an assortment of names. Suspect any omphalodes without a specific name to be this. It is about eight inches to a foot tall with milky white flowers and the usual navel-shaped seeds. Let it self-sow, it won't do much harm.

Osteospermums are sometimes *Dimorphotheca.* Thomson and Morgan sells *O.* 'Starshine' which is a good red. *D. barberae* is a very attractive pink. These are really perennial and can be kept alive in the alpine house. If you don't have a greenhouse they can be treated as annuals, but then they take longer to flower.

Petunia axillaris. I confess to having grown a petunia. One of the parents of the overbred monsters. It is a large white trumpet but not as overbearing as the F1 hybrids with candy stripes and ruffles. I just had a single specimen and not a twenty-foot border of them.

Phacelia tanacetifolia. Mauve with divided leaves, taller than *P. campanularia* which is the bright blue Californian flower you can usually find in catalogs. The desirable alpine *P. sericea* is very unreliable as a perennial, and you should always collect seed to keep it going. Some forms of this are exquisite.

Platystemon californicum. Small plant, wouldn't look bad in a choice location. This is "Cream Cups," which is descriptive enough. Another plant that "comes back."

Rafinesquia glutinosa. A white lactuca from Arizona.

Rehmannia glutinosa. A tender gesneriad from China which flowers quickly enough to be considered an annual. Magenta "scroph." Its family connections aren't certain.

Sedum caeruleum. An airy blue sedum. Not much substance but quite a bit of charm. Put it where you can see the pale-blue stars.

Silene grayi. This appeared in the Scottish Rock Garden Club's seedlist recently. It behaves like an annual, making a large flowering plant the first season and then dying. Low for a silene, a well-grown plant makes a good show. At least a foot across.

Townsendia parryi. Hard to classify this gorgeous daisy. You can expect it to bloom any time from April to November. It may or may not then die. The first bloom is usually enormous. If you remove it before seed forms it will form a bouquet of heads which bloom intermittently. If you think of it as an annual, you won't be disappointed. The name *T. grandiflora* is often seen, but is it different from *parryi*? Other townsendias may be annual; nobody seems to want to commit themselves. The possibilities are annual, winter annual, biennial, short-lived perennial, and monocarpic. Why not try several and see what they are in your garden? Put them with your most precious alpines.

Vittadinia australis. Another composite, white, to be grown as an annual unless you take it indoors for the winter. It comes from the antipodes.

This is not meant to be exhaustive by any means. It is supposed to engage your interest and calm your well-merited antipathy to a maligned group of plants. Go to the lists and instead of rejecting seed because it is from an annual, try it for that very reason. It is "something else to do."

ASARUM HARTWEGII, *middle-size ground cover.*

DICENTRA EXIMIA, *a vigorous plant for dappled shade.*

✌§ III §✍

The Philosophy of the Garden

What is Gardening?

Gardening Is Not a Science

YOU MIGHT CALL agriculture a science. In some circles you would be on very shaky intellectual ground, but much agriculture is scientific enough, especially compared with gardening. Gardeners usually have little incentive to perform scientific experiments, and they usually have too little plant material to conduct experiments even if they wanted to. We discover, innovate, experiment, but in the end our experience is anecdotal and not scientific. We try this and that but never with "controls" suitable for testing a hypothesis about correct soil texture, moisture, fertilizer, cold hardiness, rooting hormone, acidity, germination conditions, and so on. We never examine the genes of garden hybrids to aid identification of parentage. Most of us don't ever use even a hand lens to look at hairs, anthers, farina, seed shape, etc., that might identify a particular species. This would seem to be science at its most elementary, yet it is beyond our capabilities and outside our interest.

We want our nurserymen to be one step ahead of us in the science of agriculture and to pass on their know-how and their chemistry. We want our professional botanists to keep us informed about their science as it affects us. Otherwise we are content to do our one-of-a-kind trials and compare notes with other gardeners doing their own one-of-a-kind trials under totally different conditions. Very perverse. Very exhilarating. We want to find a good home for a beautiful plant. Only too often we are happy enough to exploit the adaptability of most plants to a wide spectrum of conditions. What could be tried, for example, might be an attempt to maximize the bloom on *Gentiana acaulis* by varying the chemical and moisture content of the soil, its porosity, the duration and intensity of light, the chemical content and movement of the air, etc. When you get right down to describing a scientific experiment it probably cannot be done in a garden at all.

Is gardening, then, an art?

Gardening Is Not an Art

How could it be? We all do it. What does the phrase mean, anyway? Are we talking about an art form such as drama, music, poetry, or painting? Or are we talking about the special skill of a surgeon, the grace and control of an acrobat, or the experienced savvy of a bidder at auction? Gardening doesn't fit into any of these usages of the word. You might look at Versailles or Chatsworth and, blinded by the beauty of the architecture, suppose that the grounds are also examples of an art form. Well, perhaps landscaping *is* an art form, but that activity is so debased that it now includes merely hiding the concrete foundations of a suburban house with a couple of yews and a leucothoe. Such mundane activity can't really be called art; one might as well call a house painter an artist. And does gardening have anything in common with landscaping except a partial overlap of materials and a partial overlap of intent? Is the space around Versailles a garden?

Clearly most rock gardeners try to accommodate the landscaping aesthetic when they lay out their beds, their rocks, and even when they plant out their plants. Harmonious plant associations are valued and used. At an elementary level we like to see aubrieta and alyssum flowing gracefully side by side down the face of a wall. It may be a cliché in England, but it continues to appeal as one of the boldest statements about spring's fresh effusiveness. We also try more sophisticated designs, sometimes restricting our plantings to one or two dominant colors (as in Nina Lambert's pink garden in Ithaca, and the white garden at Sissinghurst) or using colored foliage to achieve fanciful effects. I saw a fine example of this last October at a garden in Cumbria, England. This was a symphony of variegated plants with no hint of excess. But of course landscaping is not gardening. It is only the first step of a process. If landscaping were gardening, you could garden on paper, inventing the most remarkable arrangement of paths, beds, rocks, furniture, and plants. You could present your design to a landscape contractor and have it executed. But until some time had elapsed and you had been obliged to do something about upkeep and to correct all the inevitable errors of the blueprint, it would only be as close to a garden as the confections whipped up for a flower show and made of burlap, wood chips, peat moss, and potted plants. To state the obvious: a garden is an organic object—it grows—and gardening is a process. Time is one of the materials of gardening.

And can we say gardening is an art in the sense of an extraordinary skill? I suppose so, but I don't know anybody who has it. Not in the same way that an Olympic iceskater is skilled who gets a 9.5 score for figure skating or a good cook is skilled who bakes the same perfect dessert time after time. Did you ever see a streamside planting of primula at the peak of perfection? How was it accomplished? It must have something to do with location; it must have something to do with that particular season; it could have something to do with the quality of the original plants. We have all had successes that seemed beyond our just deserts and failures that nothing could explain. We know pretty well the level of our gardening abilities and find that Nature sometimes bestows on us undeserved splendor and at other times inflicts humiliating disappointment. How can we call gardening an art when chance intervenes at every turn? Is my gardening bad because the deer grazed the iberis? Is it good gardening to erect a deer fence? Maybe so. But surely hurricanes have to be held responsible for some of the damage they do, and not the long-suffering gardener. Likewise animals, drought, and pestilence may have to bear some blame for a garden's shortcomings.

Perhaps our best hope for gardening as an art is that gardening is an activity whose never-achieved aim is progress towards a never-completed work of art.

Is gardening a craft?

Gardening Is Not a Craft

Do you know any woodcarvers, weavers, or cabinetmakers? What makes them tick? They have their own materials and tools, their own traditions, methods, and skills. They need years of apprenticeship to master their crafts. All this applies to gardening more or less.

The main difference seems to me to be materialistic. The end result of a craft is usually an object with an intrinsic monetary value which bears some relation to the value of the original materials, the time taken to make it, and the requisite skill. There is an additional factor to do with aesthetics and originality and a fudge factor to do with marketability.

I don't think gardens are really concerned with monetary value. Of course we grow plants which are rare and therefore possibly valuable. We grow plants which take years to mature and flower. But these don't determine the value of a garden. Indeed a garden is so individual that its value to another person— even another gardener—is usually pretty low. Try selling your house with its fantasy rock garden on the open market, and you may find out that what is of immense value and importance to you is seen as a liability by the real-estate agent. What is the first thing a gardener does on buying a new home? Rip out the previous owner's overgrown shrubbery and start a rock garden! Or rip out the rock garden and build a swimming pool. A carved door or a pretty ceramic sink seems to be worth considerably more in the open market than a collection of saxifrages or an alpine scree.

Maybe gardening is a game.

Gardening Is Not a Game

There are elements of sport to gardening, though. Gardeners are certainly competitive. But they are as likely as not to give the game away by sharing their most precious plants. The game they play is far too chivalrous to be called a sport. Their competition is really with Nature, not with fellow gardeners. This elevates gardening to simply another aspect of living.

Sometimes a non-gardening friend will speak patronizingly of your "hobby," but you can rest assured that you are continuing a tradition dating from time immemorial that places your activity well above collecting matchbook covers or bird watching (both admirable occupations, I hasten to add). My guess is that agriculture was started by gardeners and that agribusiness was just a spin-off. The herbalists of yore probably needed the excuse of making potions and liniments to justify moving wildflowers into their gardens. And, even if that isn't strictly true, I'll wager the herbalists got satisfaction from their gardens no different in kind from what we derive from our own less utilitarian gardens.

We can safely describe gardening as simply a part of Life, with the elements of Science, Art, Craft, and Play thrown in for good measure. Gardening doesn't need to be inflated or trivialized into something it is not.

Is gardening an obsession?

Yes!

Two Gardeners

T HERE ARE TWO gardeners at war inside each one of us. Gardener Number One wants a garden with form and an easily recognizable beauty. His ideal may be Sissinghurst or Longwood, it may be a Japanese garden such as the one at Rioan-ji, or it may even derive from Versailles. In other words, a formal garden. If he is a rock gardener, Number One might aspire to a modified version of the rock garden at Edinburgh; the limiting factors would be space and cost. In any case Gardener Number One wants everything to be immaculate. The plant material should be well placed and be in harmony with the basic design of the garden. Labels should be invisible or non-existent, or they might hang on decorative chains from noble trees like the silver labels on crystal decanters that give you confidence that the wine is not cooking sherry. The plants should be of decent growth, looking as though they had lived there a long time and were thoroughly contented with the treatment they were getting. Baby plants should be out of sight in a nursery concealed behind a clipped hedge, not parading themselves conspicuously amongst their betters. The philosophy of Gardener Number One is: what is the point of growing a plant you can't grow well?

Gardener Number Two wants to grow everything. His garden is full of labels, and many of the labels are without a plant. The living plants are predominantly babies. While Gardener

Number One remembers the names of all his plants, Gardener Number Two depends on labels to refresh his memory. Even two-year-old plants need to be accompanied by a reminder, for Number Two's perpetual nightmare is to be asked the name of a large flourishing plant that has clearly been there five years and be forced to admit that the label is lost and he doesn't remember the name. His philosophy is: the world is full of an almost infinite number of plants, and I shall try to grow as many of them as I can before death intervenes in the process. As a consequence he is growing rare and difficult plants that will linger on for one season or less. As Dr. Johnson might have said, It is not well grown, but you are surprised to find it grown at all. To aid this enterprise Number Two engages in ridiculous experiments in winter protection. These never work. His garden is full of unfinished projects and has an unsettled look brought on by a half-dug bed, a half-built structure, or the beginnings of an artificial stream.

Gardener Number One mows every week; Gardener Number Two tries not to have grass at all. Both of them are compulsive about grass. Number One will mow more than once in a week when visitors are imminent, and Thanksgiving is not too late for him to be out with the mower. Number Two chips away at the lawn and will not be content until the entire property has been converted into flower beds. There are endless arguments about the relative value of a calm green framework to the garden and an ever-larger collection of plants.

The plantings in the beds also reflect the conflicting attitudes of the two gardeners. Gardener Number One has plants segregated by genus or by family; sometimes they are arranged geographically, occasionally segregation is refined to the point where all plants in a particular bed are from one particular mountain range or endemic to the Pine Barrens of New Jersey. If Number One has a perennial border you can be certain that correct color associations are in evidence and that plants will bloom at the appropriate time for these associations to be seen to fullest advantage. Moreover the texture and color of leaves is of as much importance as flower color. Number One will go to endless trouble moving plants around to conform to these

precepts. He has theories about cool and warm colors, colors
that clash, colors that give the illusion of lengthening a short
garden. He has even been known to reject a plant because the
color of the flower clashed with the color of the leaf. Gardener
Number One has strong ideas about the unsuitability of some
plants; irises, for instance, may be rejected as having no place
in the border.

Gardener Number Two grows Japanese plants next to European plants, alpines next to plants from the seashore. He places
plants next to each other without regard to color, genus, ethnic
origin, or anybody's creed. He likes magenta. His color sense
is subordinated to the need to find a place where he thinks the
plant will grow best. He is quite likely to "collect" a genus,
and if he is into rhododendrons he is unperturbed by a purple
R. Catawbiense next to an orange azalea. He may breed irises
or daylilies, in which case his flower beds will quite likely look
like a vegetable garden. The flowers, if and when they appear,
will be examined as individuals and not have their identity confused with their neighbor's. Number Two will excuse the gay
confusion of his May alpine garden by asserting that this is
exactly what plants do "in Nature." If pressed he may point to
two clashing plants that can be found growing side by side in
Nepal. He likes grey and silver plants as well as Gardener Number One, but to him they represent the adaptation of plants to
harsh conditions. He enjoys the freaks and accidents that have
provided Gardener Number One with his best material—the
good forms, the albinos, the variegated foliage, the dwarf—but
he sees them as either a triumph of the breeder's art, evidence
of a sharp eye at spotting the unusual in Nature, or quite simply
as another prize in his collection.

Gardener Number One wants his plants to look well fed,
well cared for. He wants them to provide plenty of cutting
material, to set plenty of seed, and to divide nicely in the spring.
He uses chemical fertilizer to get these results. He protects individual shrubs and trees with burlap against winter's blasts,
and he protects bulbs from rodents by planting them in wire
baskets. At great expense he erects an electric fence to deter the
deer. He has an arsenal of spray guns, herbicides, chemicals,

tractors, and chain saws at the service of his plants.

Gardener Number Two is growing so many plants and cultivating such a large area he has no time for these devices. If his plants seem undersized he says they are "in character." He remembers that most of the plants on the mountains are not show-quality specimens. If he gives a plant winter protection it is as an experiment, and he would rather not grow crocus than submit to a regime decreed by the local mice. Nevertheless he is attempting to grow borderline-hardy plants. Either they are little-known plants from southern nurseries that he wants to try out "in case they turn out to be hardy," or they are plants he has grown from seed, hoping that by some miracle of random gene distribution he will find a more or less hardy plant amongst a flush of reluctant New Zealanders or lowland Greeks.

Gardener Number One mulches to keep the weeds down. He weeds throughout the season, of course, and he also prunes and dead-heads. Dead-heading encourages more flowers and a longer period of beauty. Even if the productive period is over, Number One gets pleasure from a cleaned-up plant. This explains his negative feelings about Oriental poppies and why narcissus are "unsuitable" for a perennial border. Above all he hates all those superfluous alliums, campanulas, and rudbeckias that will invade the garden if he relaxes his program of cutting off dead flowers. Number Two does not dead-head. He wants the seed. He will send the seed to national societies, gaining donor privileges in the seed exchange. He collects seed for his own use too. Only by collecting seed can he hope to raise a new and better form of a plant he is now growing. He also wants his plants to sow their seed in the garden; what could be more delightful than a large patch of *Gentiana verna* happily spreading around? How otherwise could one even hope to get an increase in *Cypripedium acaule*? He sees the fruited plant as a mature entity, a completed episode, a fulfillment. The plant has finished off what a plant is supposed to do. No bee's work has been thwarted, ants have been provided with food, and the next generation of plants is already in progress. Gardener Number One cares little for bees and nothing for ants; the next generation will arrive by mail next spring.

Both gardeners are photographers. And even if they do not actually take photographs, their view of a garden is a series of snapshots. Number One uses a wide-angle lens. He wants to show the sweep of a lawn, the way the garden provides a setting for the house, color combinations in the perennial border, the bones of the rock work in the alpine garden, the myriad colors of the fall garden, drifts of tulips and daffodils in spring. Number Two takes close-ups. He wants a record of the one flower of *Aquilegia jonesii* he will ever grow. He wants a slide collection of all the penstemons he has raised from seed. He wants examples of all the eastern wildflowers crammed into his woodland garden. The slides will be vastly enlarged by his projector next winter and will give the impression of luxuriant color washing over the garden. He will choose to forget that on one day one plant produced one superb flower which was virtually invisible in the vast expanse of the rest of the garden. The camera and the camera of the mind miraculously and conveniently isolate its beauty and its uniqueness.

Both gardeners share their passion with visitors; Number One and Number Two unite in welcoming them to see the garden. Number One likes garden clubs: lots of people, at least some of whom will offer admiration and most of whom will recognize a good show when they see one. He will even charge admission, or at least wish that he in good conscience could. Number Two prefers plants persons. A few people, but all appreciative of an interesting plant. People who want yet another penstemon or even a hieracium; people who bring an androsace as a gift, or a rare ranunculus. And with the visitors both gardeners like to talk about plants. Some of the plants that Gardener Number Two has planted, such as *Echinocereus viridiflorus*, Gardener Number One will describe as "ugly" or "hostile." Number Two will use words such as "fascinating" and "cute." Gardener Number One, who has planted peony "Bowl of Cream," will mention it as "a perfect foil for the hot color of an Oriental poppy," or at least as a great garden plant. Number Two will mutter something about a man-made atrocity. And when they buy their plants by mail Number One will order ten of a kind, as though he needs that number to ensure a decent display, while

Number Two will order one of everything in the catalog. Number Two is curious to see them all; he wonders which will grow best, and although it is highly unlikely that they will prosper, he plans to order several more of the most satisfactory kinds next year.

Gardener Number One is a purist. He knows exactly which plants are acceptable in a perennial border. If he has a "mixed border," he grows good sound perennials and worthwhile shrubs, not a mish-mash of weeds. His rock garden contains well-tried hardy alpines. His slightly tender plants live in an alpine house or a greenhouse. He never grows annuals. Poor Number Two: half the time he doesn't even know whether a plant is annual or perennial, hardy or tender; it is probably the first time he is growing it. But in any case he has no shame. He likes annuals. He likes the ones that die off never to return because they leave space for more plants, and he likes the ones that choose to make their home in the garden because it signifies a certain kind of success. He stops short of growing petunias with alpines, but his rock garden is never without annuals.

And when they travel to the mountains the conflict between Gardener Number One and Gardener Number Two flares into a raging battle. Number One has either bought a computerized automatic sprinkler system or paid his neighbor to come and water every other day. With a carefree mind he revels in the wildness of the mountains and the beauty of the flora, he notes the rightness of the relationship between plant and habitat. Number Two feels guilty at having left his garden for two weeks. He knows his neighbor is incapable of providing even rudimentary care for his plants, and all his ongoing experiments seem doomed to failure. He observes the plants in their habitat and imagines he could reproduce exactly those conditions in his own garden. If he collects a plant with the intention of making the experiment he is overwhelmed with guilt; if he does not, he is overwhelmed with regret. He returns home from his vacation with a deep sense of relief.

Perhaps Gardener Number One is that part of us that sees Nature as the source of all beauty, while Gardener Number Two sees Nature as the fountain of all knowledge.

Taste

ILOVE PRETENTIOUSNESS. The grand gesture. The State-ment. Sometimes I feel that my own style of gardening is too diffuse, understated, diffident. There is the flamboyant erup-tion in May and June, of course, but everybody has that. You would have to work hard not to have a highly dramatic garden then. Spring makes its own statement, so loud and clear that the gardener seems to be only one of the instruments, not the composer. But I feel sometimes the need for a hundred feet of water flowing down stone steps as in the gardens at Chatsworth or a pagoda like Kew's. Or not even buildings; just an *allée* of pleached hornbeams or a topiary garden filled with elephants and huntsmen.

How I wish one of my ancestors had filched a marble from Athens or an obelisk from Egypt, or at least plundered enough wealth legally to hire an Italian sculptor to mold a set of lead shepherds and shepherdnesses. What glitter the powerful and wealthy have left for us! Without their wickedness and greed, none of these bursts of artistic energy would have been released. Can we admire Blenheim, Versailles, or even Longwood and see only the landscaper's art? Or the Ginkakuji in Kyoto? The statement these gardens make is a rhetoric only the blind could fail to recognize.

Do our own gardens give us away in the same manner? A single painted gnome sends out a message we think we can read and either tolerate or ridicule. If your immediate reaction is a patronizing dismissal of both gnome and owner, you had better examine very carefully your own trash-filled life. *Dynasty* and Disneyland are inescapable, and the gnome in the garden just might be ironic. Also it might be the lead shepherdess of the next century. I saw a garden years ago in the west of England which was filled with gnomes, owls, verse-inscribed plaques, grotesqueries of every description placed demurely amongst the rocks and plants—a tight, well-kept little garden which was generously open to casual passers-by. The public obviously vis-ited it and loved it. What was the significance of this extravagant statement? The message begins to elude you when you think about the person, a piece of whose soul is laid bare in front of you. Words like "tasteless" are merely buzz-words of the patronizing. Taste can only handle ideas within a local, contemporary canon; you have to know the rules before you can pass judgment on whether a particular Italian garden or a particular Medieval cloister is tasteless. We don't use such strong language about historic or exotic manifestations. To do so would be tasteless. Or pretentious? Is Mount Rushmore tasteless? Do you have to know the life history of the subject and the motive of the artist before you can use words like "tasteless" and "pretentious?"

These thoughts are not irrelevant to visitors of gardens. Some gardens came into existence to honor or flatter a man; and some gardens are comparable to a cathedral added to over many years by different people with different motives. Others display the horticultural ideas of a single mind. Our own gardens should not have to suffer such convoluted speculation in the minds of our friends and visitors. Everybody feels his own garden is unself-consciously "just a garden." Psychoanalysis on the basis of one's scree or woodland is out of place. But you can't help thinking that there must be something written there, if only you knew how to read it.

Hierarchies

THERE ARE HIERARCHIES of all descriptions: wealth, power, goodness, beauty, intelligence, fame, strength, influence. Every sport and every skill has its own pantheon, priests, acolytes, and camp followers. At the bottom, the unwashed millions who pay no attention to the pronouncements, laws, and shenanigans of even the gods themselves.

At the hoi-polloi end of the gardening hierarchy we get condominium owners, apartment dwellers, and other folk without a garden. Next, the deprived people who have yielded their rights or have yet to earn them: babies too small to dig, the aged and infirm too feeble to lift, children and spouses of gardeners for whom the light is not yet revealed or for whom access is denied. Then there are the people with enough space who nevertheless have to use it as a parking lot or a playground. These people are in limbo. Consider also the people with space whose garden is a dumping ground for all the objects the house cannot or will not hold: broken artifacts, half-finished wood-work, a doghouse. These last are in purgatory.

Descending farther into these depths, we find the millions who live their lives vicariously, horticulturally speaking. Their house lot has been subjected to low-maintenance landscaping, or they live only vaguely associated with someone else's garden, and they feel it would be inappropriate or uncongenial to enter the garden except to get to the front door. These are the damned.

Finally we come to the people who actually garden. At this point we slide inexorably towards controversy and contentious-ness. Hierarchies are notorious for competiton and infighting among the ranks. Parallel structures in the same establishment are often at loggerheads. In politics opposing parties exhibit bitter opposition at the appropriate times but will unite against another group, especially a one-party system. Religious hier-archies make evangelical forays into the territory of their rivals but close ranks against the identifiable heathen.

Hierarchies of intelligence and athletics show off their rank with degrees and silver cups that separate the sheep from the goats. Great singers deride each other's abilities, and opera and pop singers barely acknowledge each other's existence. This branching of hierarchies is a common phenomenon as the tree of status rises to its giddy heights.

Take gardening. Vegetable gardeners and ornamental gar-deners branch away from each other fairly low on the tree. They seem to be linked by herb gardeners, who have their own hierarchy but are little admired by either of the other groups. The ornamental crowd splits into those whose ultimate aim is parks and those interested in landscape. Another group is the flower people, with strictly tree and shrub types falling midway. Flower people divide into the indoor and outdoor crowds, the glass-house/windowsill group splintering into partisans of or-chids, succulents, "houseplants," cactus, and so on. These groups are sufficiently subdivided to form national societies with local chapters each with its own hierarchy. The outdoor gardeners also split up. Some are perennial growers, who themselves rise in hierarchical status by becoming one-genus types. A further refinement splits off the plant breeders into a higher cast.

At this point I shall stop describing hierarchies lest I become judgmental and betray my own prejudices. Not that I care too much about word getting around; if you come to my garden you can see for yourself what my prejudices are and fit me into your own favorite hierarchy. I would do the same for you.

Many of us are installed in several hierarchies. In some we have upward mobility, in some we have a noticeable downward trend. Gardeners may not fight each other with the vigor of associate professors or United Nations representatives, but they certainly proselytize as subtly as a bishop. Every time you give a lithops to an orchid grower or a bearded iris to a rock gardener, you are engaged in an effort to change the recipient's way of life.

You may think that you are just tossing out surplus plants. That may be only your way of minimizing guilt feelings. The evangelistic effect is still there.

Most of us are suckers for any plant and willing to give a home to the most unsuitable gifts. So it follows that you should never emphasize the faults of the plants you give. Plants can speak for themselves. If you know something really bad about the plant, pass the information along by all means, but as information, not as discouragement. Otherwise why give it? If you move over from one hierarchy to another leave your old love without regret, without ridicule, and pass on your love to a friend without much criticism. As they used to say before homogenization: when you give a glass of milk never take the cream off the top.

The Meanings of Flowers

YOU MUST HAVE seen those books, so popular earlier this century, which assigned a significance to a flower for the purpose of conveying a wordless message. The books, usually illustrated with a wealth of watercolor drawings, were presumably aimed at the bouquet-sending crowd. Many of the messages were sinister and uncomplimentary, however, and it is hard to imagine a personal relationship that included both send-

ing flowers and an insult via the same messenger. I expect the
books were really designed for the consumption of people who
believed there were other people who did these things. Rather
like *Dynasty* on a more subdued plane.

Everybody has his own flower associations, and here are some
of mine.

Allium for Loyalty. There are great societies for the worship
and sexual harassment of primula, iris, hosta, lilium, even penstemon. None that I know of have been set up to idolize allium.
Yet allium has devotees every bit as loyal and devout as those
of the better-known religions. At the 1985 Western Weekend
we were enchanted by Mark McDonough's display of affection
for this genus. We had a full hour of photographs, information,
and proselytizing. Since I was well on the way to conversion
before the talk, I could allow myself to indulge in a side emotion
of admiration for Mark's evangelical skill. Truly the Billy Graham of the onion world. Another acolyte resides in a remote
corner of northwest England. Dilys Davies grows more than a
hundred species. In fact she is the doyenne of allium preservation
for the Hardy Plant Society and displays the same moving loyalty that Mark does for alliums in the United States.

Carex for Far-out Taste. I once asked an eminent botanist if
any member of the floral kingdom still had the ability to please
and astonish one whose whole life had been spent with plants.
I expected him to admit that any plant could still quicken the
pulse. Instead: "if I happened across a new sedge I would be
very happy."

Opuntia for Circumspection. Anyone who inadvertently grazes
a cactus with a careless gesture of the hand will quickly learn
circumspection. The ultimate lesson was learned by Timmy
Foster as a child when careless hand was transferred to the mouth
and instantly produced a lifelong aversion to all cactus. I still
grow opuntias, but Timmy's misfortune flashes through my
subconscious each time the bed needs weeding.

Phyteuma for Doubt. Long ago the Connecticut chapter of the
American Rock Garden Society hosted a joint meeting with the
Long Island chapter at which Bill Brown gave a talk on easy
plants for the beginner. One of these was *Phyteuma comosum*.

Dianthus chinensis for Family Unity. I can't see this annual without thinking of an English brother-in-law who visited a Canadian sister and took back a few seeds to be grown. The seed was then harvested again and again. Each year full reports went back to Canada. I think of seed from a plant in my garden as mine, but Tom still calls the dianthus "Phyll's pinks."

Lewisia for Collectability. There are few genera of which anybody can claim to have all the species. Lewisia is possible, and Kath Dryden did it. We visited her garden and saw the collection of Lewisias ready for display at the next Chelsea show.

Kniphofia for Pride. My mother never bragged. But she did have a stand of red-hot pokers to be proud of, and she counted the blooms each year, reporting the ever-increasing number in the next letter. My youngest sister now carries the torch.

Phlox nana for Charity. The only time I ever contributed money in connection with a flower was for *Phlox nana*, so that the photograph of a scarlet form found by Paul Maslin could be reproduced in color in the ARGS Bulletin.

Draba mollissima for Ingenuity. This plant is not one for the open garden in the northeastern United States, and since it is a hairy bun of great character it is a favorite alpine houseplant and custom designed for a March or April show. One year Paul Halladin showed *Draba mollissima* in full flower in May to everybody's delight and astonishment. When asked how he had managed to preserve the flowers that late in the year he confessed to dressing the pot with ice cubes every day for a month.

Hymenocallis for Barterability. All bulbs are tradable. They can be sent unobtrusively by mail across international boundaries if need be, with nobody the wiser. Garry Newton exchanges his own etchings of hymenocallis for hymenocallis bulbs, the barter supreme.

Adonis amurensis for Generosity. I have received many plants from fellow gardeners but no gift was quite as touching as a division of this precious plant from Norman Priest. At the time I was a beginner and a newcomer to the Connecticut scene.

Johnny-jump-up for Guilt. This was a gift I had to refuse. There was a tray full of plants, and the giver was a dear neighbor. I even said: "We throw those away." I still blush inwardly at the memory of my behavior in that ungracious episode.

Aubrieta deltoidea for Remembrance. Particularly a lovely double from Carol Sienko. Many plants have personal associations, but Carol was the first visitor to the garden who wasn't just a neighbor or a relative.

Trillium grandiflorum fl. pl. for Memorial. Different in meaning from the last as I didn't know John Osborne personally. When he died Judy Glattstein distributed divisions of his celebrated double trillium to many Connecticut gardeners.

Campanula piperi alba for Devotion. A plant of this rare campanula was discovered by Steve Doonan in the Olympic Mountains of Washington State. Instead of digging it up, Steve remembered the spot and went back next year to fertilize it.

Aesthetics and Etiquette

SINCE EVERY ROCK garden is to some degree an expression of the interests and personality of the gardener, it would seem that there was nothing worthwhile to say about garden aesthetics. We all know that gardens quite different from our own can be appealing, uplifting, even moving. Other gardens may have an aim and style that is somehow not to our taste. When our own garden is visited by a friend or a stranger we want it to be liked. No matter how firmly we assert that we garden only for ourselves, we *still* want it to be liked.

Art teachers are of two schools. One teacher will start you off drawing cylinders and cubes from life and gradually work up to figure drawing, with the help of lots of rules about what is usually called "technique." Another teacher will give you free rein and supply more or less cogent criticism that assumes you really know what you want to do but need pushing in the right direction. I recall two nuggets from two different teachers that may have application in the garden. One teacher constantly complained of "dirty edges." If an area of oil paint had a ragged look which served no useful purpose, out came the reproof: "Your edges are dirty." This can be all too true in gardening; the edge between garden and non-garden should be clearly defined. That means the line between grass and soil, grass and path, path and soil, patio and grass, scree and patio, etc. Plants can extend over the line to break the hard line. You can also merge two areas, or rather use one area for two purposes. Example: the patio and scree may adjoin and be of one kind of stone. But if there is a line, it has to be a *clear* line. A raised bed or a bank can define it too. The principle of clean edges means that a really weedy path is a no-no, because you just don't know which is garden. Lawn weeds creeping into the garden give the same kind of dirty effect. On the other hand a large plant of goldenrod in the middle of the bed can sometimes be overlooked completely. The aesthetic sense ignores it.

Another teacher would constantly refer to the "spaces." We would be figure drawing and having trouble getting an elbow correctly placed. Her idea was to draw correctly the gap between the arm and the body so that the parts fell into place. This is of no direct use in the garden, but there *is* an idea there. When you are making a new bed or changing the shape of an established bed, stop a minute to look at the shape of the lawn you are leaving behind. If you make a path through the garden, look at the shape of the areas you have left for the beds. If you are placing a raised bed look at the "sea" around the island. You have to walk around it; is there room? It often helps to look at the garden's "spaces."

Color is a vexed question in gardening. There are many people for whom gardens are simply exercises in color patterns, with flowers as the sometimes unwilling material with which to work. These are the people who aim to have a blue-and-white garden, an all pink, or a yellow-and-orange display. Or they may be "flower arrangers" who grow mostly greenish or brownish flowers. They are often very assertive about which colors may not be adjacent. Or they may dislike white flowers. Rock gardening does not lend itself to such fantasies. We are not growing great globs of reliable old *Campanula glomerata* or sheets of lemon daylily, and the arrangement you can perpetrate with violet petunias and orange marigolds which, once achieved, will last the better part of three months is out of the question. Our androsaces and drabas are not reliable, blend with any other rock plants which happen to be out, and have a relatively short season, often quite early. Color is never much of a problem in a rock garden. People who tell you that such and such a plant is hard to place are carrying over inappropriate criteria from another ballpark. The only kind of rule that makes sense is one that says that a very bright color next to a less-bright color may have the effect of allowing you to overlook a perfectly beautiful but noncompetitive plant, and this would be a pity if the plant unable to assert itself were *Codonopsis ovata* or *Disporum flavum*. Also, it is sometimes difficult to distinguish between two neighboring white plants in full bloom, and thus the effect of each is diminished. There is a fillip, though, from plants of the same color with different form or texture standing as neighbors.

Nature made most plants yellow, magenta, grey-blue, or white. The bright reds, deep blues, and rich purples are natural rarities. It is a little absurd for a rock gardener to have a strong aversion to yellow, magenta, dirty blue, or white. Yet one reads constantly of these ridiculous airs and graces. If you really want to play around with color, you can plant many different shades of reds and magentas and get a magnificent effect. It can be a *tour de force*, but I don't think it has much to do with rock gardening. For one thing the tiniest oxalis weed can shatter the effect. More to the point, if you are going to treat plants as paint pots you really should grow large groups of large plants. The impact of even *Daphne cneorum* is minuscule when used paint-pot fashion, much less that of *Androsace mathildae*.

Nevertheless many people will assert that this or that color flower is unappealing (mostly magenta, I believe). If you are one of these unhappy types who finds *Silene acaulis* without charm, it may pay to examine your dislike rationally and search for a good psychological explanation of what after all is merely dislike of a wavelength of light. Dislike of yellow or magenta could arise from its association with some terrible weed (goldenrod? oxalis? fireweed?). More likely dislike of magenta will turn out to be a holdover from all those garden books which told you not to like it. I won't dispute your aversion or presume to explain it, but you would be a lot happier discarding it.

For one thing you would not be as candid as the visitor who looked out of my kitchen window at a dearly loved rhododendron P.J.M. and said "I hate that color." Which brings me to etiquette. Would Miss Manners have said that? When we show our gardens we don't need extravagant praise so much as understanding and appreciation of our achievement thus far. Extravagant praise is also nice. So when you look at a garden don't say 1.) "Do you really grow that thing?" 2.) "I have a better form," or 3.) "I hate that color." Instead say something nice, like 1.) "Would you save me some seed of that?" 2.) "That reminds me of Lincoln Foster's garden," or 3.) you know what else.

What Friends Are For

Do you have the kind of friends that offer Constructive Criticism? Is the opposite Destructive Praise? Which is worse? A friend in England has a cottage garden behind a fifteenth-century cottage. A neighbor stopped by one day and remarked: "I love your garden. It's such a jumble."

Color

WHAT COLOR IS *Primula vulgaris*? One author says yellow, another sulphur-yellow, and a third cream-yellow. Is *Mertensia virginica* cool violet blue, or purplish blue? What about *Callirhoe involucrata*? Cherry red? Crimson? Magenta? Are the bracts of paronychia silver or dingy white?

We have three sources for our concept of color: one of them is physics and the study of light; another is the painter's palette of pigments taken from nature and augmented by chemistry; the third is color as a visual quality to be described in subjective terms by the observer using language of common-sense comparison, poetic analogy, folk metaphor, or the hyperbole of advertising. Most of the time gardeners are concerned with the third mode of description, but it is helpful to realize that the first two modes exist.

The primary colors of light are green, magenta, and orange. Mixtures of these lights produce other colors of the spectrum. The painter regards red, yellow, and blue as the primary colors.

A mixture of pure red and pure yellow gives orange, and the other secondary colors, green and purple, are also obtained by mixtures of two primary colors. If all three primary colors are mixed, or if two secondary colors are mixed, a modified primary, a modified secondary, or some form of brown or grey is obtained. In practice pigments are made from natural dyes, clays, or chemical substances ground into a fine powder and mixed with oil or some other medium. None of the pigments are "pure" colors in the same sense that the wavelength of light can be manipulated to give a "pure" color; rather, the pigments are the results of mixtures discovered empirically. Complicating the discussion is the fact that in painting black and white must be thought of as colors. As far as light is concerned, however, black is absence of light and white the combination of all the colors, in that white light can be obtained by combining any color with its complement. But there is no combination of pigments that will yield white paint, and so this color is made from zinc- or lead- or titanium oxide. Similarly black paint is made from lamp black, and only an approximation to this color can be obtained mixing other pigments.

We can name a monochromatic light color without ambiguity by referring to the wavelength of the light. We can refer to a pigment in its pure form by describing its origin. For instance gamboge and viridian are both well-known colors, as are ultramarine, burnt sienna, and so on. Not only are these colors fairly standard from manufacturer to manufacturer, but mixtures of them have been prepared by artists for centuries, so that a well-trained eye can recognize many of the pigments seen in paintings throughout history.

Flower colors obviously cannot be described either in terms of wavelength of light or pigment mixture. Instead we use rather general names such as "red," "pink," and so on. This leaves us with the rainbow color names and the diluted versions of them. Violet and mauve are possible examples. If you think about any of these commonly used names it is clear that each name stands for a whole range of color. Red diluted to make pink could "contain" a little green and thus be on the brownish side, or it could be on the "blue side" or the "orange side of the spectrum."

The quotes here indicate that since we are not either speaking of transmitted light or pigment the phrase is only metaphoric.

Madison Avenue has grappled with the problem of color names for years. The solution there is to describe a color as "raspberry" or "chestnut," which bypasses finding a color name and offers instead an object with a similar color. We are left with two new problems: locating one of the objects named (persimmon, cocoa beans, etc.), and deciding whether the state of the object (ripeness, variety, age, etc.) we have found affected what the color namer had in mind. Do you know what crushed blueberry would be? Or pebble? Garnet? Another, related method of identifying color is to invent a name and plug it with examples until it becomes a household word. Remember "Shocking Pink," "Princess Margaret Rose"? "Navy blue" has been around a long time but clearly not forever.

Standardization of color names has been tried, but no scheme is generally accepted. For instance the Royal Horticultural Society put out color swatches some years ago hoping to achieve uniformity in plant descriptions. I have seen a few references to plants blessed with a color name from this list, but there is no general acceptance of such a standard. I think the reason is we don't want to pin down colors too carefully. We carry around a collection of color recollections. The blue of *Campanula rotundifolia*, the yellow of solidago, the yellow of *Linum capitatum*, and so on. But the blue is "almost grey" and surely contains "mauve," and the two yellows are quite different. We would perhaps resort to metaphor to indicate the difference; Solidago is "heavier," "more strident," "duller" (does it in fact contain more black?). The linum is "clearer," "fresher," or more near to "lemon" (back to the analogies). Reds cause even more problems, as everyday English is totally inadequate to describe the red–blue part of the spectrum. The word "red" can include any color from orange to purple, blue taking over from there. Purple, magenta, violet are all ambiguous names from this region and are used almost indiscriminately by gardeners and writers alike. Add dilutions of these colors, and the whole range can be summarized as "pink." For some, "pink" is not even a dilution.

There seems to be no answer to the problem of color names, but as in much of gardening one accepts life's limitations as part of the game. Perhaps the name of a color has really less importance for plants than for lipstick or scarves or hair dye. The plants in the garden are seen in many colors of light. The soft orange as the sun sets on an August evening, the strong blue light of a clear noon in April, the romantic moist grey of early November. The color of a flower changes in different lights and also in different contexts. What a difference a mass of white makes to an otherwise dingy pink. A mauve nepeta amongst a group of alyssum changes yellow into gold. Dead brown petals among the lush pink of a peony create an unsettling, almost unhealthy look that can induce a bout of dead-heading. The feeling can be so uncontrollable that gardeners without clippers sometimes try unsuccessfully to decapitate by hand.

And how have taxonomists handled the problem of naming colors? A fascinating discussion of the subject is presented in Stearn's *Botanical Latin*. Color names are needed for the official description of a plant, but many specific names of plants are color names, and it is interesting and useful to recognize such names when they are attached to well-known plants. Some examples are *Erigeron aurantiacus* (orange); *Crocus aureus* (golden yellow) or its new name *Crocus flavus* (pale yellow) *var. luteus* (pure yellow); *Campanula lactiflora* (milk-white flowers); *Iris atropurpurea* (dark purple); and *Primula luteola* (light yellow). But presumably these names are assigned to distinguish a particular species from others of the genus, not necessarily as pure description. How else would you explain the name *Dictamnus albus var. ruber*, which isn't a real hearty red and certainly isn't white? Also botanical names don't clearly refer to flower color, e.g., *Iris crocea* (saffron color), or leaf color, e.g., *Zauschneria cana* (greyish white).

The subject is full of emotion and immersed in imprecision. Gardeners do not want to pinpoint likes and dislikes, prefer using terms like "garish," "strident," "bright," "subtle," "dingy," "vibrant," and "muddy" to indicate that at this time, in this place, in this mood, by this light, they do or do not like the color of this, especially next to that. Without color we might have as many words for form as we now have for color.

Uniqueness

SOMETIMES AFTER WE drive away having visiting a garden, every sentence either begins "If only. . . ," or "I'm glad . . ." If only I had a stream, if only I had a ledge, if only my garden were finite, if only I had more space, if only I had those magnificent maples, if only I had a place for a bog, if only I had an alpine house—ad infinitum. Or the other demon raises its head, I'm glad I don't have tree roots, I'm glad I have a bit of shade, I'm glad my garden is well drained, I'm glad I don't have equisetum, at least my garden never floods, and we don't have black fly!—again ad infinitum. In other words we constantly compare what They do with what We do. If you are piercingly self-analytical and just a wee bit truthful you recognize a hint of envy and a soupçon of smugness. Then you analyze the situation and resolve to change your garden or stick it out the way it is, or simply move house. A garden visit can be a disturbing–exhilarating experience.

I would like to muse over the uniqueness of every garden and suggest that you look at your own with a fresh eye. Let's first dispose of obvious macro-distinctions between gardens. My garden is not like the convent garden I used to overlook in Alexandria, Egypt, full of palms and tropical evergreens—a garden that never went dormant. Nor is it like an English garden with its long, drawn-out spring which sometimes never quite becomes summer and a winter of never-ending threats and promises. I don't have the rain and the slugs of Washington State or the arid heat of Denver. New England is unique in the world as far as I know—maybe northern Japan might come close.

So let's narrow it down a bit further. I can't grow the same plants in Southwestern Massachusetts that I used to grow on Long Island. *Helleborus corsicus* would never bloom here, nor would many of the azaleas which glorify Long Island in May survive our winters. Even gardens as close as a hundred miles north or south have slightly different climates. Fifteen miles away, Norfolk, Connecticut, is colder, Winsted warmer. Now look at gardens close to your own. Some on a hillside, some flat, some in woodland, some in cities. Even two neighboring city gardens have differences of light caused by building shadows. When I had a garden behind a New York City brownstone, the sun came into the garden at 9:15 A.M. on the longest day of the year and left at 3:20 P.M. My next-door neighbor had a few more minutes.

Your garden is like nobody else's. Those variations in light, drainage, exposure, fertility make it unique in the same way that a human body is unique. We can rejoice that diversity is one of the givens of gardening. Now add the variation that the gardener imposes on the given environment, and you have the equivalent of a life history written in muscles and wrinkles on the human body—and I suppose jewels and paint correspond to bird baths and deck chairs. And it is easy to see that the only way you can have the garden you just visited is to engineer a quick sale on the way out. Apart from that you can only take away ideas. Back home you have to fit the ideas you came away with into the constraints to which your unique piece of real estate is subject. And sometimes it can't be done.

Glory in this uniqueness, but recognize that it comes with a price. Only *you* know the quirks and the horrors, the gifts and the hidden virtues of your garden. There is nobody out there with all the answers to its unique problems. Try to be as independent as the Czech botanic garden whose tests of rhododendrons over a ten-year experimental period completely ignored hardiness ratings from outside sources. We must do even more complicated experimentation. If a plant fails in the textbook location, try it again and then again, and then try it in a different location and maybe still another. Okay: you may not want the plant that badly.

I have tried *Phlox adsurgens* in scree and in woodland and in habitats between, some places more than once. I have had good seasons but not mastery. I know it can be grown because Linc Foster grows it. But there is nowhere in my garden quite like the steep, shady, moist hillside at Millstream, and in any case which aspect of Linc's success is the crucial one? It may be his soil for all I know, and nothing to do with light or moisture. *Silene hookeri* is another mystery plant which may be "tender," or short-lived. At least I know it can survive some winters here, but never, it seems, two consecutive ones. I shall keep trying

SILENE HOOKERI. *Very beautiful and fickle; the true plant is hard to find.*

with both these teasers. Could it be the gardener and not the garden? Don't you smile at the English sometimes when they talk about "my heavy clay" in describing a success or a failure? Is that really the crucial factor? Could it be that people like Linc have a lot of luck? *And* a unique garden?

Religion, Politics, Sex, and Other Taboo Subjects

IT WOULD BE most unsuitable to discuss the paraphernalia of these subjects in a short essay. Party, dogma, and other preferences are reserved for private—even intimate—conversations. A borderline topic of conversation is one's own health. Only if asked are you allowed to describe it and maybe even discuss it, otherwise the topic is taboo. But why is this the case? Can't we be more outspoken, at least about gardening diseases? Perhaps a seminar should be arranged to pool the special information that has accumulated from doctors, mothers, herbals, or even trial and error about our special ailments. Weeder's wrist, spade knee, raker's shoulder, transplant finger—all could be finally eradicated. There might be a workshop on extraction of foreign bodies from the extremities, with special attention to thorns, hairs, and fibers. Another on stings, bites, and scratches with hands-on use of witch hazel, baking soda, and all the favorite salves, sprays, and ointments our medicine chests are full of. Yet another group would discuss the ways and means of repelling or obstructing live flying objects by bee hats or unguents. How about an exchange table so that we can unload the remedies which don't actually work. We need to publish a pamphlet, too, which warns against all those hostile plants we learn about too late: the bristles on onosma leaves, the bracts of acanthus, euphorbia sap, the wicked points on penstemon seedpods, and the hairs on opuntia which are even worse than the spines. Too often the only plant warnings are on seed packets claiming that a plant is poisonous, as if we care. Do you go around tasting plant parts?

Another seminar could discuss friendly plants. Do any of our members understand the curative properties of the plants we grow? Whatever do you do with borage? Does *Pulmonaria* 'Mrs. Moon' work just as well? Has anyone made a brew from the roots of *Gentiana lutea*? One of my worst childhood memories is being forced to drink lukewarm gentian tea after a spell in bed with an upset stomach. Would *Gentiana tibetica* work as well? I would love to get that one out of my garden.

But consider the really taboo subjects. Sex, for example. You can't describe half the species we grow without some naughty reference. At one time the shape of the plant's sexual parts might even disqualify it for entry into plant shows. Remember thrum-eyed and pin-eyed primulas? I can't for the life of me remember which kind was preferred. And anatomy matters too. You can tell a lilium from a narcissus by finding its ovary. You wonder if there isn't a better way. Some worrisome questions are conveniently forgotten in the garden. Like sex without procreation —isn't that what dead-heading means? Or procreation without sex—should we really take cuttings so lightly? And layering?

As gardeners, we find politics is constantly nagging us at every turn whether we are partisan or apolitical. Are you a devout environmentalist? Do you throw your support to the chemical industry? What about gun control, animal rights? The garden is a crucible of practical politics. If you are a preservationist do you only plant the wildflowers of your area? Do those wildflowers really belong where you put them or are you creating an "unnatural" environment for them? Is it better to plant a sarracenia in a man-made bog than to bulldoze it to make a parking lot? In the long run the plant is doomed anyway. In the macrocosm of world insanity our small depredations seem insignificant, but they haunt us just the same. Gardeners are not destroyers so much as busybodies. We say to the birds: yes, do come and eat my viburnum berries, if possible after Thanksgiving, but on no account eat the crocus flowers. Butterflies are welcome; their babies are not. Animals: keep out. My dog: Yes. Your dog: No. Worms: Eat. Ladybugs: Stay—sorry, I just sprayed your dinner. If you start thinking about animal rights you start wondering whether to have a garden at all.

The metaphor of Adam's ouster from the Garden of Eden is very powerful. Any ecological system which includes man is already on a course to self-destruct. This line of thinking is anathema. Politics and religion must include gardening. But my garden is itself a temple, with no priests, no dogma. We are sometimes visited by small groups of evangelicals who leave tracts if discourse is discouraged. Once they asked to see the garden and after a half-hour the conversation went: "What beauty God has made!" "Not at all, *we* spent ten years making this garden." And of course both views are correct if you interpret the words to suit your religion or lack of it. One thing that unites all gardeners as they contemplate the compost heap is a belief in reincarnation, at least for plants. Here we have a microcosm of decay and vitality. The bottom line for us all.

Help

Do you work your own garden? I mean fetch and carry, dig and rake for yourself? Or do you have a "gardener once a week" or a nephew who drops in? Or does the local garden club come in to do your weeding because "they admire your writing so much" or for some other odd reason? Not to be censorious (because I am sure there is nothing immoral about having help), but it must be obvious that a garden with more than two hands on the keyboard is that much less of a virtuoso solo. Really big gardens seem to be the work of a committee. An orchestra?

I am a little afraid of having help of any kind. If the help is intelligent, artistic, or knowledgeable every move requires endless discussion and argument. If I get my own way there is no satisfaction, as I have to justify my decisions to somebody who has nothing but some nebulous prestige at stake yet I am still faced with "I told you so" if the decision turns out wrong. When I do follow advice, however, it is with such reluctance and disaffection that I botch the transplant job or resent the color combination. If the help is strong-arm or comes with a piece of equipment I don't own but need, the whole day can be wasted watching that the job is done properly. If one tries to mind one's own business one is on pins and needles wondering if one should be overseeing the operation. If you don't watch there is always something done wrong.

There are, of course, certain jobs done by people loosely called "professionals," where none of the above anxiety obtains. You may get a tree removed or a lawn mowed with little apprehension and no argument; but even elementary jobs like these require a good deal of preliminary discussion about the direction of the fall or which is grass and which alpine lawn.

As time goes on this state of affairs culminates in a series of unpleasant choices. With advancing age one feels less and less inclined to do everything the garden requires. One choice is to yield territory, to give up the conquest of yet more pasture and woodland, to retreat gracefully from land previously won. Another choice might be to fall for low-maintenance propaganda; this probably means changing the design of the garden. Or you could hire a person or persons to carry out your ideas, and so replace gardening with supervision. Finally you could hire a "landscape architect" who would take away your pleasure in gardening finally and completely, replacing care of your love-child with inactive ownership of a changeling, a brainchild only partly yours that is fed by a steady flow of cash. Such a garden ends up being "low maintenance" mainly because the landscape architect will not cooperate with your hare-brained, labor-intensive schemes so lovingly half-baked that only a gardener could dream them up.

Each of us solves the problem of gardening help in his own way. I have no idea which route I shall take, and perhaps it is useless to chart a route before you need to. A garden will have its own effect on our decisions; the lilac you planted fifteen years ago may be at war with a raised bed. At the time you built it, the bed seemed remote enough from the lilac for all aesthetic and horticultural purposes. Perhaps the moment of truth crept up on you gradually as the plants in the bed died or grew out of character; perhaps you have a premonition that something unpleasant might happen if you fail to remove your favorite lilac. Gardens abound with these confrontations. A visitor may wonder aloud at your lack of foresight in planting a lilac so close to a raised bed of alpines, failing to understand the historical context and its annual procrastination and deferred action. Your landscape architect would deal ruthlessly with the problem. Sentimentality creates dilemmas, and your weakness merits an indulgent smile. Destroy the raised bed, and chop down the lilac, too.

Think a long time before you hand over your garden to another. Remember how unconcernedly you removed the leggy ilex when you took it over from the previous owner, even though he assured you it was a rare form grown from a cutting stolen on a visit to Longwood in the late fifties? Better to get the strong-arm in than endure the inhumanity of Mr. Thickskin Architect. On the other hand deep down we know that a clean sweep is just what the garden needs occasionally, and perhaps it is best to pay to have it done.

I think about retreating as often as I think about dying. When something is inevitable, you do what you have to do. It isn't necessarily pleasant. The problem of giving up even part of a garden is a little like asking, "would I want to go on living if . . ." The answer is usually yes. Especially if you put in a whole bunch of provisos. But *in extremis* the answer would be no. And with a garden, too, if all work had lost its savor and the nephew moved away, you might want to hire a team of upkeep types to run around once a week. A tear falls at this gloomy thought. I shall hope to die digging.

Some Conflicts

GARDENERS ARE PRACTICAL people—most of the time. All ideologies, philosophies, and religions take a back seat to the overriding imperatives of Nature. We may or may not believe in a deity, but we certainly don't trust Him/Her to water on schedule. We exhibit the complete spectrum of conservationist behavior from organic to chemical, all in the name of Practicality. We raid community leaf dumps, sawmills, chicken farms, riding schools, and cocoa-bean processors for waste products to enhance the soil. And we regularly apply 10–10–10 and slug bait, Roundup and other lethal sprays. Whatever the activity, we always say we are just being "practical." Gardening being largely trial and error, no one bothers to challenge this.

Gardeners are also a bunch of mystics. Even the downright irreligious have to contend with the mysteries of life and death at a very down-to-earth level. Biology and horticulture sometimes attempt to explain these mysteries but in the end often offer only partial answers to our questions. No Final Answer. Are there *any* simple answers? The questions seem more imponderable the further you get away from vegetable gardening. I always think vegetable gardeners have an easy time. Lots of writers take care of their needs. For a rock gardener mysteries abound, and our attempt to resolve them is often tentative and inconclusive. We do indeed need knowledge to grow plants, but it is knowledge often not to be found in books, and sometimes our gardening techniques border on art and the occult. Books and people help, of course, but the complete answer remains elusive.

This practical/mystical dilemma is not the only conflict a gardener faces. Another struggle that afflicts the souls of all of us is the contest between greed and generosity. Caught at the

right time any gardener will give you seed, a cutting, a transplant, a division, even a tree. Not just for the asking, but because
of some wish to share the munificence of Nature, or to share
the joy of growing things, or for the beauty of the gift itself.
Actually asking for something is usually a turn-off; the way to
get a plant is to show interest and admiration, not unvarnished
desire. The obverse of a gardener's generosity is his greed. Every
gardener knows this greed. I heard a man looking at a group
of plants say, "I have all the plants I need." Ridiculous. He said
it because he was leaving for South America next day, and he
didn't have his checkbook, and it was December and he didn't
have a cold frame. To gratify my acquisitive streak, I part with
hundreds of dollars each year to nurserymen scattered all over
the country and a few from abroad. I rationalize my extrava-
gance by an argument that runs as follows: only nurserymen
can supply me with thus and thus, so it behooves me to keep
this person in business. Both parts of this argument are true;
there are many desirable plants in this world, and each nursery
seems to have a few that I cannot live without. Here is a plant
I know to be rare and difficult to propagate. Only a small profit
can be made by the grower. I must purchase it to help him
survive! This is pure sophistry. The reason I buy plants has
nothing to do with charity. My true motive is closer to the
passionate greed of the antique collector or bibliophile, greed
close to pathological. Under extreme duress a gardener has been
known to steal a cutting or even dig a plant in a national park.
This cannot be condoned, although each of us understands.

A third conflict shows itself in simple physical activity. It
could be called a conflict between laziness and energy, but that
would be an oversimplification. If a gardener has a job to do,
the task can become a Categorical Imperative. This guarantees
abundant feelings of guilt if the timing or standard of perfor-
mance fall short of the targeted goal. The job may be preparation
of soil, irrigation, winter protection—anything can trigger this
sort of obsessive behavior. And most gardeners really want to
do a good job, sometimes for aesthetic reasons, for a spiritual
feeling of sacred obligation, for their friend's approval, even for
the sake of history. The conflict is brought on because we realize

this excess is both unnecessary and unwarranted and therefore morally incorrect. As a consequence we look for ways of making the job easier or shorter. We plead that we must not allow gardening to become an obsession, we even take a vacation. Weeds multiply, the vital project gets postponed, the pruning is left until next February "when there is nothing else to do." Is it laziness or common sense? A non-gardener is contemptuous of the dilemma. But it will not go away. Each year I leave my garden for two weeks, or even two days, ostensibly on a pleasure jaunt, and return to some catastrophe that my conscience tells me could have been averted if I had stayed behind. Each year too I labor to extend the garden to new and distant territory, or I become interested in a brand-new aspect of gardening. In other words I prepare a burden for myself that I know may very well aggravate the conflict of the active/passive demons of gardening. Don't you do this? The gardens I love most are the ones whose owners are trying to stretch their capacities to the limit and where the garden itself says "look at me as an ideal, not as an actuality." A finished garden is on its way to becoming an abandoned one. A satisfied gardener has already stopped gardening.

Another conflict concerns modesty and pride. The paradigm is the professional athlete who walks a fine line between natural joy at winning after demonstrating his skills and turning off his audience by an excessive display of hubris and arrogance. The other side of the coin is the person who thinks everything he can do is easy and trivial and whose modest disclaimers begin to sound bored or just wimpish. The extremes make us feel uneasy when others indulge, but in fact we all brag, and we all belittle our activities.

And what about the scientific/aesthetic conflict? At times we take potshots at the wildflower people who use common names for plants, and we put down the gardener who is too interested in color combinations or flower arranging or topiary. We say they aren't true "plantspeople." At other times we flaunt our own rock-garden aesthetics and end up confusing beauty with rarity or difficulty. Sometimes we set about collecting all the available species of one genus, aspiring to a pseudoscientific dream of completeness. Then our aesthetic angel takes over and obliges us to discard the weedies and the uglies.

How do we endure these conflicts? Do you consider yourself practical, greedy, lazy, scientific, mystical, generous, energetic, modest, aesthetic? It would be hard to deny being all these but probably unwise to pigeonhole oneself into any of these boxes; they are all vices if overindulged.

Does "Pleasure" Bring Happiness?

I HATE PLEASURE. Cocktail parties, air travel, silk underwear, late-night banquets, lying on the beach, ring-side seats, disco music, and anything jolly. I'm not especially puritanical; that word doesn't come close to describing or explaining my negative feelings. Nor am I other-worldly, ethereal, or whatever you want to call indifference to the five senses. I just don't think the common notion of pleasure retailed by the ad-men and enforced by peer pressure comes close to whatever it is that makes me happy (whatever that means).

Being happy is dirt under your fingernails, wearing old clothes, having a good idea get better the longer you work at it, starting a new bed, giving plants away, and listening to rain. Returning from a picnic a friend said, "You know when you have had a good time when everybody is itchy, querulous, bloated, hungry, sunburnt, and sleepy." I know *I* have had a good time when my shoes are full of grit, my hands chapped, my legs tottering under me, with a slight twinge in my shoulders, a shooting pain at the back of my neck, wet knees, and chipped nails. It is dangerous to try to explain your pleasure to anyone else, especially a non-gardener. Their kindest comment is: "You must have worked hard." There is no point in describing an ecstasy which disfigures one's hands and ruins one's clothes. No point in showing a weeded bed—they had no idea what it was like before. No point in showing a bed under construction—they do not regard this heap of dirt as the first stages of an altar to the Goddess Flora. No point in trying to explain why one is limping or has cracked lips and scratched hands. You would be chided or ridiculed.

ASARUM CANADENSE, *an easy wild ginger for shade and woodsy soil.*

Gardeners must take their pleasure where they can find it, often alone; their high points are little spots of color, tiny oases of neatness, a whiff of perfume, hairs on a leaf. None of the components of normal, everyday pleasure.

Pleasure is all in the mind. Such a cliché. But think about its possible meaning: only intellectual stimuli give pleasure. Obviously false, but the intellectual component of gardening is nearly always in the background. Consider the sense stimuli from a mound of *Dianthus erinaceus*; a greyish-green prickly lump with few and modest flowers. You have to be pretty close to the ground to even notice it. You need to have developed a very sophisticated yardstick for form and color to appreciate it, and as you admire its compact, austere beauty, your mind is engaged in subconscious explanations of its form, comparisons with its relatives and its neighbors, enjoyment of its rarity and its "difficulty." And then your fingers take in the provocative minor-league hostility of the leaf endings. Just think of a garden full of experiences to match this one and you realize exactly why happiness is here and not at the beach, the ballpark, or the cocktail party.

❧ IV ❧

Mixed Seeds

PRIMULA CARNIOLICA. *Grow all Auricula species of primula
from seed or from cuttings.*

Seedlists

THE ENGLISH LANGUAGE has many *lacunae*, gaps where a word is missing that exactly describes a particular situation or event. Germans have an easier time with their modular combinations that construct new ideas out of stale material. *Schreibzeugkistenhandler*, if it were a word, would mean a person who merchandizes boxes of writing materials. Germans would know what the word meant, though they might disapprove of it. A very simple missing word in English is one to describe the emotion/attitude/personality of a person with a passion for seeds. Chocolate lovers have plundered "alcoholic" to arrive at "chocoholic," however, and by extension we might summon up "seedaholic." But it would not have the same connotation. By now we associate a physical disease with the word "alcoholic," and so "chocoholic" is reduced to a comic analogy with about the same derivative value as "superette" and "laundromat." "Seedaholic" is even further removed from an acceptable etymology: it seems to describe a person inordinately fond of poppyseed pastry, halvah, or sesame-seed buns. But there is a trait in some rock gardeners only incompletely described by "greed," "addiction," "passion"; it combines all these and goes even further. Collecting matchbox covers or Picassos might involve greed, addiction, and passion, but it might also involve elements of ownership and aesthetics absent from the seed fiend. Instead there would be elements of curiosity and anticipation, and indeed the seeds themselves would have value only insofar as they represented a stage on the way to plants. Vintage seed has little value, and so any analogy with either alcohol or Picassos fails. In April last year's harvest is non-tradable except to the desperate, the gullible, and the indifferent. By November the previous year's seed has revitalized value; we sow our leftovers to "test for viability," "as an insurance policy in case the first crop fails," "to have a few more plants to trade in the spring," etc. There are many rationalizations. The truth is that we sow last year's leftovers in November because we want to be in there sowing seed, we want something to do that reconnects us to the life cycle of a plant. The net result of these November old-seed orgies is a vast array of pots that fail to germinate and a few pots that give us hundreds more plants of species we already have enough of. Just occasionally a pot will germinate that replaces a first sowing lost to the weather, to animals, or to carelessness.

I used to think I was unique in my affliction, but I have met others with similar symptoms. What shall it be called? An ailment? It is no more an ailment than jogging to a high or collecting silver you have no intention of using. A disease? Certainly it is not infectious. Some people stand unmoved by packets of seed and rows of pots. Their only comment is: "Whatever will you do with them all when they germinate?" If it is a disease immunity is commonplace. Passion? Close, but there is no orgasm. The climax of the activity is a slow succession of isolated ejaculations spread out through the spring as one pot after another germinates. The follow-up sequence, being the raising of plants, is as mundane, binding, and disappointing as child rearing.

And of course not all the pots germinate, by any means. To continue with the sexual analogy, many titillating encounters are nonproductive. In fact for the seed maniac that is the norm.

How does a seed person obtain seed? There are many sources, all worthwhile. The first and most obvious way is to take them from a plant. But whose plant? Every gardener has a garden, and seed is there for the taking wherever bees are doing what bees do. Just hit the right day when the seeds are ready to collect. I won't describe what this means. It is as complicated as trying to tell a non-cook how to tell when a custard is ready. You have to read a lot and listen a lot to know which seeds are sown "green" on the spot and which to gather thoroughly ripe, which seeds can ripen in a paper bag and which must stay on the plant until they are ready to pop, which seeds are safe to leave a few days and which seeds pop and disappear forever if you are an hour late, which seeds ants will carry away without fail and which seeds even the birds disdain in mid-winter. But all this is a different kind of mania. Seed collecting is itself a disease. Collectors have the same nutty-nice quality as those amateur gourmet chefs who cook for their friends. Seed collectors will walk thirty miles in a day with paper bags and labels. They will bump across rocky dirt roads in four-wheel-drives. They will get caught in the first snowstorm of September in the Big Horns. They will suffer mountain sickness and enteritis in Kashmir and Turkey.

These collectors are purveyors of seed to keepers of seedlists. List makers provide menus from which we seed people choose our feast. There are many kinds of seedlist. The commercial, the botanical garden, the society seedlists, the wildflower societies, the specialist societies, and the personal seedlists. It is immoral to generalize about these groups, but I shall do so anyway. You must sift out the truth.

First, you can get errors in *any* seedlist, even from the most august sources. Seedlist errors are as easy to make as any typographical error, but there are other "more serious" errors unique to seedlists. One of these is wrong names, i.e., not just an obsolete name or a name of "no botanical standing," but a mistake as glaring as *Silene acaulis* seed labeled *Campanula piperi*. They just put it in the wrong packet. Or something else happened that has an explanation and demands an apology. No hope of that, but every seed person must be prepared for mistakes. A commercial outfit is less likely to make a really outrageous error because they are presumably handling large batches that resist getting mixed up. Botanical gardens might be expected to be error-free in their nomenclature (they are not), but the same careless error could be made by a seed collector in a botanic garden as by you in yours. Enough needling. Both these kinds of lists are in fact reliable on the whole. The fault of the commercial lists is that they are unadventurous, and there is little variation from one year to the next. If there is an interesting species listed, the supply has run out when you order it, or there is a "crop failure." I nearly always order some seed from commercial sources. The record of germination is a little better than with other sources, but not much.

How different are the botanical gardens? You find many unfamiliar names in their lists, but typically the plants turn out to be weeds or at least non-ornamental. Sometimes a treasure is lurking there, but botanical gardens are more interested in research than in horticulture, and many of the plants turn out to be local lowland wildflowers of little merit or grasses and pulses

whose primary interest is as food or fodder. At first I thought
it would be fun to grow quantities of "new" species, but after
a few burdocks, hawkweeds, and oats I am a little wary of
research material. Each botanical garden has many sections, and
if you get a list restricted to rock-garden plants that is a joy
indeed.

You can get partial satisfaction by becoming a member of
the Royal Horticultural Society and obtaining the seedlist of
plants grown at Wisley. The range is very broad, and the list
is relatively short, so unless your tastes are catholic you might
find the bounty illusory. There is always something good, though.
Next come the lists from the great societies; the American Rock
Garden Society, the Alpine Garden Society, the Scottish Rock
Garden Club, the Alpine Garden Club of British Columbia,
and the Canterbury Alpine Garden Society. There may also be
many European and Japanese societies with which I am unfamiliar. The seeds for these lists are collected by the members
in the wild and from their own gardens. There is a wide variation in the knowledge and experience of the members, and
the lists are reliable but not 100-percent so. With hundreds of
contributors there are bound to be errors of all sorts. We can
live with that, but there is always an element of chance in sowing
the seed. Naturally it is expected that mistakes in naming will
be rectified and not perpetuated by the people who grow the
plants and collect seed to send to the exchange again. Occasionally a mistake becomes widespread, however. A few years
ago every packet of *Silene hookeri* from all the exchanges turned
out to be *Lychnis flos-jovis*, a pretty enough plant, but hardly
the choice and temperamental silene. Lately gardeners are wise
to the error, and recent listings of *Silene hookeri* have been genuine. These big seedlists are a labor of love by a few enthusiastic
volunteers. Often the love is strained a little by members with
character defects ranging from normal human weaknesses to
the worst excesses of seedaholism. There are always a few people who complain because they didn't get their first choices or
their full quota—usually people who haven't followed instructions. The Postal Service also creates its own brand of chagrin
for the unfortunate few. All in all, the seedlists are the pride of

the societies and keep the loyalty of many members.

The specialists societies also have lists. The wildflower societies usually list seeds from native plants, so if you want to grow desert plants, woodland plants, or whatever, you have to find and join the society for wildflowers in that state or region whose flora interests you. The object of most wildflower societies is finding and identifying flowers in the wild, preservation, and conservation. Not every society will think it part of its job to disseminate seed to the rest of the country. There are other specialist groups concentrating in the genera *Primula*, *Iris*, *Penstemon*, *Hosta*, and *Rhododendron*, to name a few. All have societies to study them and grow them. Part of growing a single genus is the fun of hybridizing. This is a world apart, and you may or may not get the bug; even if you don't hybridize, you can share the hybridizer's pleasure by selecting

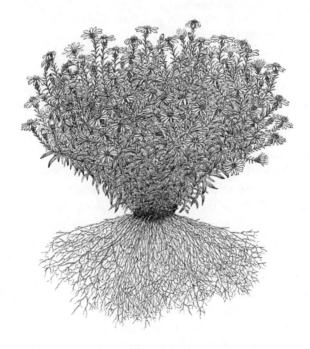

ASTER LINARIIFOLIUS. *The stiff aster forms a tidy mound for early fall.*

good plants grown from their seed and propagating them vegetatively. There is always a subgroup of members interested in
species. I have never fallen for hybridizing but have grown
hybrid penstemons with enthusiasm. I suspect that at the back
of every hybridizer's mind is the hope of a cross that will shake
the horticultural world with its panache; it will be hardy from
Zone 3 to Zone 8, vigorous but not weedy, easy to propagate,
scented, and exquisitely beautiful. It will bear the name of the
hybridizer's mother or a favorite dog. White Flower Farm or
Wayside Gardens will snap it up for exclusive propagation at
enormous prices. The hybridizer cannot be hoping for great
financial gain, for there is only a remote prospect of that, but
it is an extension of one's life-span to have a plant of one's
creation to leave to the gardeners of the future. Like having a
child who can't talk back.

The specialist groups hold up another carrot to the horticulturally gullible: the prospect of growing all the species of a given
genus. *Penstemon, Primula,* and *Iris* are genera very rich in variation. They all have species differing in form and cultural needs
and covering a spectrum of plants for border, scree, woodland,
even bog (exclude penstemon). Each year the seedlists tempt
one to grow yet another member of the genus. You could grow
a hundred different penstemons or primulas if you had the space
and skill. Many of the species are difficult, and some are impossible in some locations. There are some species such as *Primula flaccida* that I have failed with each year for ten years. I still
think it worth the effort to try again. I don't want to appear
too starry-eyed about this project of growing "all the species."
After years of looking at new species you become a little disappointed that they are not all equally beautiful and, worse,
that they are not always different enough from some other
species to be distinguishable from five feet above ground level.

Horticulture and botany are uneasy bedfellows. We gardeners
fear the lumpers because they diminish our collections. Remember the outcry when *Lewisia heckneri* was demoted to being
a mere form of *L. cotyledon*? This meant we were growing one
fewer species. Also we think (wrongly) that *Daphne mezereum*
and *D. mezereum album* should be separate species, not merely

different forms. Isn't it plain? But equally the splitters cause us problems, by encouraging us to grow plants that have no horticultural distinction despite having different names. Look at the swarms of drabas with their enticing names that turn out to be the same little yellow buns allegedly differing in the shape of the hairs on the stems. But our complaint about botanical splitters is, at last, foolish and only exposes the willful blindness of most gardeners. We refuse to look beyond what is visible to the naked eye at five feet—three feet for a flower show. And with what eyes! We start gardening too late in life when the visual experience has already begun to blur and dim, and the beauty under the microscope eludes us.

Finally there are the private seedlists. I only discovered these within the last year or so. You really need to "know" a few Czechs and Germans to get the full benefit, but once you start a correspondence with avid rock gardeners you receive all kinds of lists of seeds either collected in the wild or from plants grown in their own gardens. I send all my surplus seed to the main exchanges, but there seems to be a tradition in some countries of sending around lists including as many as a hundred or more species, often very choice plants. By the time I have ordered seed from four commercial sources, three botanic gardens, ten societies and wildflower groups, and fifteen correspondents, I am not only in seventh heaven, I am swamped with seed. This year after promising to retrench I sowed 1,900 packets again. They are not all new species. Some of them are species I want more plants of (any douglasia, for instance), and some are variable enough to warrant growing them again and again (*Primula elatior*, for instance), and I continue the search for a freely flowering *Silene acaulis*. But most of the species I order each year are new. There is no thrill so great as seeing a new species emerge from seed, produce its first leaves, and ultimately flower. By the time you have grown 2,000 species you could believe you had exhausted Nature's imaginative variability; by the time you have grown 5,000 you realize you never will. There is always something new. This is what my kind of gardening is all about.

"Jack"*

This is the seed that Jack sowed.

This is the plant, a tight little bun,
That came from the seed that Jack sowed.

This is the cutting, rooted in sand,
(Potted in compost prepared by hand)
That came from the plant
That grew from the seed that Jack sowed.

This is the hole in the rock-garden bed,
At the back of the house by the little black shed,
Where the cutting was planted, rooted in sand,
That grew from the seed that Jack sowed.

This is the spade that dug the hole
In the rock-garden bed quite close to the wall
At the back of the house by the little black shed
Where the cutting was planted, rooted in sand,
That came from a plant from a faraway land
That grew from the seed that Jack sowed.

This is the friend that gave him the spade
(And a flat of seedlings as part of a trade)
That dug the hole in the rock-garden bed,
At the back of the house near the little black shed,
Where the cutting was planted made from the bun,
That grew from a seed just sown for fun,
That Jack sowed.

This is the crowd where Jack met the friend
(Who made a raised bed just to follow the trend)
That gave him the spade (that Jack really wanted)
That dug the hole where the cutting was planted.
It came from a bun that grew from a seed
That Jack sowed.

This great society (never endowed)
Has in it the group, not much of a crowd,
Where Jack met the friend who gave him the spade
(The friend was a member with all dues paid)
That dug a hole quite close to the wall
For a cutting he planted, rooted last fall
Taken in summer from this little bun,
Grown from a seed just sown for fun—
So Jack said.

This is the seedlist bringing good cheer
To every gardener at this time of year
That belongs to ARGS (if his dues are paid)
In one of whose chapters Jack got the spade
From a member friend who shares his goal.
It was with this spade he dug the hole
And planted the cutting rooted in sand
That came from a plant from a faraway land
Grown from a seed whose name was there
(Printed in Latin to make it quite clear)
There in the seedlist (published each year
By a great society (never endowed)
For Jack and his friends, they are quite a crowd)
And Jack is a member, Jack has a friend,
Jack makes a raised bed, follows the trend,
Jack plants alpines, tight little buns,
Grown from cuttings, grown for fun;
Jack gets seed, whatever's allowed
Exchanges his plants with the rest of the crowd,
Like you.

Optional: Change 'Jack' to 'Jill'; adjust gender.

* Printed as the Introduction to the American Rock Garden Society's 1984 seedlist.

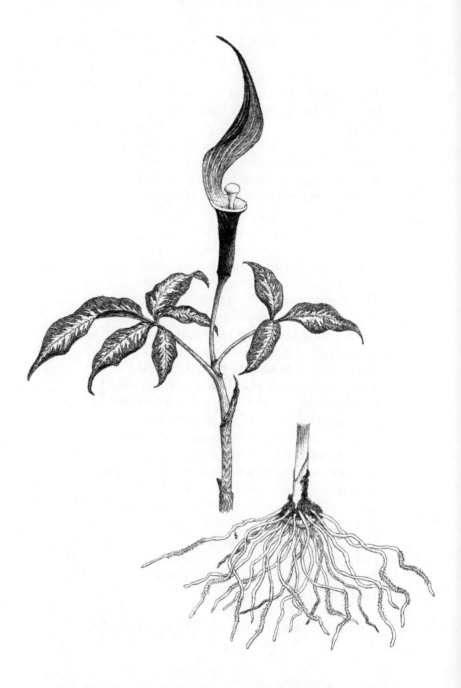

ARISAEMA SIKOKIANUM, *a spectacular Japanese aroid.*
Its name has the neuter gender.

Rock-Garden Latin

THERE ARE TWO major fears of every rock gardener when talking about plants with another rock gardener. The greatest fear is that we shall forget a name. Everybody forgets, young and old, old-timer and tyro; even professionals forget. It has nothing to do with age—well, maybe a little—but it certainly is not symptomatic of the onset of a dread disease. We know this because forgetting is so localized in time and space. We sometimes forget a crucial name that leaves a sentence hanging limp in the air refusing to crystalize. Later, when we are not struggling to form a sentence, names parade freely through our minds lined up at attention to service our thinking needs. But we stand before a *Silene acaulis* and try to tell a friend its name, and our mind goes blank. My own explanation is that gardeners load up their minds with disconnected pieces of information in greater quantity than at any previous time in their lives. Disconnected ideas refuse to be reconstructed by logic, and remembering is reduced to brute force.

If forgetting names makes us appear senile or oafish, then getting the wrong endings makes us look barbaric, as though we don't care, or illiterate, as though we didn't know. Normally we try to communicate with each other using some kind of mutually acceptable grammar, and we look askance at any slip. When it comes to botanical binomials we also try hard to obey certain rules, but sometimes the rules are obscure, and sometimes we unknowingly repeat another person's errors. We often rely on a name's "sounding right" before we dare utter it.

This second fear is really not very serious. Nobody really cares if you say *Campanula barbatum*; you would obviously be understood. If you care about getting the endings right, however, you might like a few rules to hang on to. The rules can be as hard to remember as the names, so they may not be worth the trouble. In any case I shall weasel out of full responsibility for them by reminding you that I am neither a botanist nor a linguist; the rules below are mostly distilled from William T. Stearn's book *Botanical Latin* with help from *Hortus Third* and the *RHS Dictionary*. If you are familiar with the rules, stop reading; what follows is meant for those new gardeners who knew as little as I did a couple of years ago. The only part of

Latin which need concern a rock gardener is the binomial associated with a plant. The first name in the binomial pair is the genus, and the second the species. Since Latin is an inflected language, the endings of words change to affect meaning. In our case the species name is an adjective modifying the genus name, and the ending must be chosen to agree with the genus name. The genus has one of three genders: masculine, feminine, and neuter. There are only two things to know in forming a species name: what is the gender of the genus, and what is the ending of the species for that gender?

There are "standard forms," as follows, for the genus and for the endings of the species name: feminine names and adjectives end in *-a*; masculine names and adjectives end in *-us*; neuter names and adjectives end in *-um*.

EXAMPLES: Feminine, *Campanula barbata*
Masculine, *Dianthus alpinus*
Neuter, *Delphinium grandiflorum.*

This is quite straightforward. Now for additional rules and exceptions. We will start with rules for the gender of the genus. The word "all" is used hereafter to signify "all the names you are likely to meet," "all except a few exceptions," "all I could find in my sources."

1.) Feminine names having other than the standard *-a* ending. All names ending *-e*, *-as*, *-es*, *-is*, *-os*, *-ys*, *-o*, *-ex*. These mostly come from the Greek. It is comforting to realize that nearly all the non-standard endings fall into this group.

EXAMPLES: *Androsace alpina, Asclepias tuberosa, Omphalodes linifolia, Lychnis coronaria, Rupicapnos africana, Stachys lanata, Plantago argentea, Carex pendula.*

EXCEPTION: *Senecio* is masculine—*Senecio adonidifolius.*

2.) A name is usually feminine if it ends in *-a*. If the name ends in *-ma*, however, it could be a Greek word and neuter.

EXAMPLES: *Aethionema, Phyteuma, Dierama, Onosma, Pachyphragma* are all neuter. These are the most important names; there are very few others we are likely to meet.

Thus we have: *Aethionema armenum*
Phyteuma comosum
Onosma nanum
Dierama pendulum.

3.) Names ending in -*i* are neuter.

EXAMPLE: *Thlaspi montanum, Muscari comosum.* The only two I could find.

4.) No rule for names ending in -*ops*, but there are very few.

EXAMPLES: *Echinops sphaerocephalus* and *Euryops acraeus* (masculine), but *Lithops* is feminine.

5.) Names ending in -*on* are difficult, too. Here is a shaky rule: Regard all of them as neuter except *Erigeron, Endymion, Penstemon,* and *Ophiopogon.* These four are masculine.

EXAMPLES: *Acantholimon armenum, Platycodon grandiflorum, Dodecatheon pulchellum, Hylomecon japonicum.*

EXCEPTIONS: *Erigeron compositus, Penstemon barbatus, Ophiopogon japonicus.*

6.) Names ending in -*er* have to be memorized:

Aster is masculine: *Aster alpinus. Papaver* and *Acer* are neuter: *Papaver alpinum, Acer japonicum.*

7.) Names ending in -*ax* are impossible.

EXAMPLES: *Bolax glebaria* and *Galax aphylla* (feminine); *Panax trifolius* (masculine); *Dipidax triquetrum* (neuter).

8.) Although names ending in -*us* are usually masculine, all trees ending in -*us* are feminine!

EXAMPLES: *Cornus florida, Juniperis rigida, Malus floribunda, Pinus aristata, Prunus maritima, Rhus typhina, Sorbus americana, Taxus baccata, Fraxinus americana, Euonymus japonica, Fagus sylvatica, Ficus aurea.*

EXCEPTIONS: It would be great if the rule was that all trees were feminine, but others follow the previous rules. So we have: *Acer japonicum, Rhododendron racemosum, Viburnum grandiflorum, Daphne tangutica, Ilex crenata, Chamaecyparis pisifera, Salix reticulata, Larix decidua.*

These rules and examples cover most of the genera rock gardeners usually meet. Try to fit new ones into the scheme either to fit a rule or as an exception. The examples chosen are mostly well-known plants; if you consistently get these names correct use them as models for other names formed similarly.

Spelling species names, as well as gender endings, is tricky. This is because there are so many ways of forming a specific name, and it is not always clear which method is being used.

1.) "Regular" adjectives end in -*a* for feminine, -*us* for masculine, and -*um* for neuter names. These names can indicate habitat, origin, or some quality of the species.

EXAMPLES: *Hutchinsia alpina, Dianthus alpinus, Leontopodium alpinum.*

2.) A variant of this rule is when the masculine ends in -*er*, the feminine ends in -*ra*, and the neuter in -*rum*.

EXAMPLES: *rubra, ruber, rubrum; glabra, glaber, glabrum. Fritillaria nigra, Helleborus niger, Verbascum nigrum.*

Other adjectives like these are: *pulcher, florifer, scaber, asper.* The corresponding feminine names would be: *pulchra, florifera, scabra, aspera.*

3.) Some adjectives end in -*is* for both masculine and feminine and -*e* for neuter.

EXAMPLES: *campestris, campestre; mollis, molle; perennis, perenne.* And some names of geographic location: *canadensis, canadense. Aquilegia canadensis, Allium canadense; Lupinus perennis, Linum perenne.*

4.) Comparative adjectives end in -*or* or -*ior* for both masculine and feminine, but in -*us* for neuter.

EXAMPLES: *major, majus; interior, interius; longior, longius; elatior, elatius.*

Primula elatior, Alchemilla major, Antirrhinum majus.

5.) Some adjectives are the same for all three genders. These are sometimes participles (*repens* = creeping), sometimes nouns used as adjectives.

EXAMPLES: *bicolor, sessile, bryoides* ("like moss"), *rupicola* ("rock dweller"). Any specific ending in–*oides* ("like"), -*ens* (present participle), -*icola* ("dweller") is likely to be the same for all genders.

Rhododendron rupicola, Achillea abrotanoides.

6.) If a species is named for a person, that person's name is usually in the genitive. Usually add -*ii* for a man. If the name ends in -*er* add -*i*, and if the name ends in -*y* or a vowel add -*i*. A name originally classical could end in -*i*. Also, some names break the rules. For female names add -*ae*. Sometimes a plural -*orum* is found.

EXAMPLES: *Tulipa batalinii, Tulipa sprengeri, Tulipa vvedenskyi,*

Mimulus lalyneae, Omphalodes luciliae, Cortusa matthioli. The six-teenth-century Italian Matthiola must have called himself Mat-thiolus. Another way of forming a commemorative epithet would be by adding *-ianus* to the name. The name would then be an adjective and agree with the gender of the genus in the normal way, for example: *Geranium robertianum.*

7.) Epithets can be the same for all genders if they mean "of a place." Also if the species name is that of another genus.

EXAMPLES: *Podophyllum emodi* ("from the Himalayas," which the Greeks called "Emodus").

Aster nova-angliae ("of New England")

Paradisia liliastrum (*Liliastrum* is a genus name; the ending is not changed to match the feminine *Paradisia*)

Agastache foeniculum (the Latin name for fennel)

Hacquetia epipactis (like that genus, an orchid)

Daphne mezereum (Mezereon, the common name for this plant, has been Latinized but does not get a feminine ending)

You may agree that there are too many rules and too many exceptions, but we have to accept the historical situation as it is. The invention and elaboration of the binomial system is a miracle of international scientific collaboration. If the system had to be perfected before it could be put into use, it would never have gotten beyond the first committee. If I had to do it from scratch I would scrap gender completely, but there I show a cultural bias which few Europeans would share. To gain support for my revolutionary tendencies, I would exhibit the recent change of name from *Phyteuma comosum* to *Physoplexis comosa.* The poor, unsuspecting plant underwent a gender change from neuter to feminine. Plants being for the most part bisexual, gender seems a most inappropriate and artificial attribute. Peace, Linnaeus.

Idiotic Mnemonic

Repens and reptans are rooting and creeping;
By runners sarmentosus is rooting and leaping.
Ascendens, adsurgens nearly upwards are shooting;
By stolons stoloniferus is running and rooting.

Descendens grows downwards, decumbens is flopping;
Erectus straight upwards, cernuum is dropping.
Procumbens, humifusus, and patens are spreading;
Diffusus in every direction is heading.

Deflexus bent downwards, reflexus bent backwards;
Inflexus bent inwards, convolutus rolled up.
Revolutus rolled backwards, involutus rolled inwards;
Secundus one-sided, calathinus with cup.

Villosus' long soft hair is growing old;
Hirsutus' unshaved beard is coarse and bold.
Hispidus bristly with a two–day growth;
Strigosus, hirtus, sharp and rigid both.

Silky sericeus flaunts its fine smooth hair;
Arachnoidea cobwebbed like a spider's lair.
Ciliatus' leaves like lids of eyes have lashes;
Fimbriatus fringy like Edwardian sashes.

Tomentosus' thick short hair you stroke;
Velutina's velvet on Queen Mary's toque.
Incanus hoary white, a plant for shows;
Thick wool on lanatus longer grows.

Like baby hair pilosus short and sleek;
And here's pubescens, downy, dense and weak.
Crinitus' long soft hair's in little puffs;
Barbatus is mustachioed in tufts.

Keying It Out

To a non-botanist identifying plants can be a very frustrating and mysterious procedure. I feel a certain reverence in the presence of a taxonomist. They *know*. And when they don't know, they know where to look to find out. And the tool they use looks so simple yet contrives to baffle the tyro. Just a collection of true-false questions! You look at the plant in front of you and ask yourself: are the stamens exserted? are the leaves obovate to lanceolate? There is even a glossary of botanical terms to ensure your success. One botanist friend said, to my astonishment, "You can always come up with something." I was on a round robin in the Penstemon Society for several years. Many Penstemon aficionados don't bother to grow penstemons but just spend their summers looking for them in the wild. In the middle of a long description of a hike through the Rockies comes the inevitable discovery of a penstemon and the phrase: "I keyed it out, and it turned out to be *Penstemon procerus ssp. tolmiei.*" How do they know? I can see the *Penstemon* part. But *tolmiei*??

I thought it would make identification in the garden easier for the beginner if I published a short key that even a child could use. So go into the garden, pick a flower at random, and key it out yourself.

(1.) Plant with blue flowers   (go to) 2
     Plant not as above   (go to) 6

(2.) Flowers like bunched
     soda water bottles.   *Physoplexis comosa.*
     Flowers are not as above   (go to) 3

(3.) King of the Alps.   *Eritrichium nanum.*
     Not King of the Alps.   (go to) 4

(4.) Poppy family   *Meconopsis sp.*
     Some other genus   (go to) 5

(5.) Plant refuses to flower.   Could be *Campanula zoysii.*
      Plant not as above   Could be *Myosotis sp.*

(6.) Plant with red flowers   (go to) 7
      Plant not as above   (go to) 9

(7.) Is it October?   *Zauschneria californica*
      Not as above   (go to) 8

(8.) Is it May?   *Tulipa sp.*
      Not as above.   Your plant is probably not red but
                              some shade of magenta

(9.) Plant with yellow flowers   (go to) 10
      Plant with white flowers   (go to) 11

(10.) This is too large a group for certain identification.

(11.) The *Alba* form.

Names

EVERY SO OFTEN I am engulfed by a wave of irritation over the naming of plants. The theory is beautiful. Learn the binomials: the genus (first) name gives us an instant mental picture if we already know other members of the genus, and the specific name often adds a descriptive memo to identify the species. The names are universal, so we can name a plant in Japan and the Japanese gardener will know exactly which plant we mean. I had this experience in Italy, where I watched a gardener transplanting. The only word we had in common was *Helleborus.* We both smiled knowingly.

In practice names can be a snare and a delusion. First there are so many. The mind reels at the sheer number of correct scientific names for plants, and then disbelief sets in on discovering reams and reams of rejected names, duplicate names given in error to the same plant for one reason or another. *Primula veris (L.)* has thirty-one synonyms! Many rejected names are still in current use, so plants may have two or even three names in books we are likely to have on the shelf. Examples are *Silene alpestre* = *Heliospermum quadrifidum*, and *Scilla hispanica* = *Scilla campanulata* = *Endymion hispanicus*. For many gardeners, taxonomists rank high on the public-enemies list. The very rules of nomenclature that promise clarity, fairness, and universality end up being responsible for confusion, instability, and distress. The scientists have clay feet; they are not only vain, they are sloppy. Gardeners know this can't be true, maybe the taxonomists don't have enough clay on their feet.

What about the "accepted" names themselves? Perhaps they are descriptive of the species, but sometimes occult knowledge or a vivid imagination is needed to make the description useful. Does *Campanula rotundifolia* have round leaves? Is *Corydalis lutea* the only yellow corydalis? Does *Clematis occidentalis* come from western United States or western Asia? Sometimes knowing a bit of Latin or Greek highlights one's ignorance.

Now take *Primula farinosa, P. frondosa,* and *P. algida.* I have grown all three plants from seed. As usual some labels get lost, and there comes the moment when the seed is ripe. Shall I collect seed and send it to the seed exchange? A new and beautiful book has just been published, *Primulas of Europe and America*, Smith, Burrow and Lowe. I open it avidly, believing that finally my identification problems are over. Alas, the descriptions of all three primulas are very similar, they are filled with escape words such as "usually," "not markedly," and "rarely," so nothing is final and each plant I have fits all three descriptions. The killer comes in the description of *P. algida*: "This species is intrinsically so variable that . . ." That settles it. I shall probably spend the rest of my life not knowing one from the other.

In order to feel moderately confident about the names of the plants you are growing, you should choose, from any seedlist, seeds that are known to have been collected in the wild. Seed collected in any garden is more likely to be misnamed. Species differences do occur, after all, because of geographic separation, and it isn't likely (possible?) that a collector will find *Primula algida* in Europe or *P. farinosa* in the Caucasus. If it turns out there are visible differences I will be happy to grow all of them;

if not, small botanical differences are not really interesting enough to worry an ordinary gardener. What I suspect and hope is that truly different species have a quality difference that doesn't interest a botanist but is obvious to a gardener.

And now that I have aired my own frustrations I want to emphasize how important it is for gardeners to use the correct name for their plants. It is especially important not to pass on a plant or seed with the wrong name. You can avoid the problem and the associated guilt if you label with a query such as *Primula ?algida*, or use *Primula sp.*, or *Primula (Farinosa section)*. It is very discouraging to get seed from a seed exchange and go through all the painstaking work of raising plants only to find a year and a half later that you have raised a changeling.

If you are a beginner try not to be worried about the name problem. You will never know all the names. Nobody does. At least if there are such people they don't have time to garden. Learn the names of plants as you get them, if you can, then read about other plants in the same genus to give you an idea of the remarkable differences which do exist within a genus. Just think of *Primula viallii, P. japonica, P.denticulata*, and *P. vulgaris*! All alike in an almost mystical way, yet all miraculously different. The botanists may hide behind their dry descriptions, but truth is often more beautiful than science.

Labels

THIS PIECE COULD turn sentimental, even mawkish; it could be libelous or indiscreet. You would think there could be no conceivable danger over an innocuous subject like labels. The labels in my gardening life have been in a state of steady evolution, from the days when I was content to write "Dotted Swiss" and fully expected to remember forever that this marked a large bearded iris with white markings on a blue ground, to today's practice, which crams onto a label as much information as it will bear. The other day I offered a plant to a fellow gardener and was chastened to be asked to explain the hieroglyphics. I don't think it was the requested information so much as an assurance that my signs and symbols really meant something.

For a mathematics teacher it is essential to know what a student really wants to know when he or she asks a question. This is useful at any time but especially so in a classroom situation. The intent and the "level" of the question must be estimated in a split second to avoid talking above (causing embarrassment), or talking down (causing resentment), or wasting time on a joke (causing mirth). So when the visitor asked what the hieroglyphics meant I simply parried the question by saying it was just a record of the source of the seed. An understatement.

A new world of label language opened up a couple of years ago when Anita Kistler introduced me to the Pilot pen. At the time this seemed to solve all the basic problems of permanence and practicality. The Pilot writes on plastic, dries instantly, and is waterproof. Incidentally it sometimes fades in unexplained ways after a year, whether due to sunlight or other factors I haven't yet determined; so I am not endorsing this product except to say that I still use it. Anita's most telling comment was that with a Pilot pen you can write three lines on a label. And indeed the point is so fine that this can easily be done. These pens write smoothly in their youth with the black very visible, but the essential benefit is the three-line capability.

Three lines allow room on the label for genus, species, source of seed, and whatever else seems important. Ideally a label ought to state a plant's genus, species, subspecies or variety, country of origin, and height above sea level in its natural habitat. Color, height, and breadth of the plant, flowering month, and brief cultural conditions should also be given. If the plant was grown from seed, the label ought to reveal the origin of seed and whether it was garden- or wild collected, annual, biennial, or monocarpic. The date of sowing, germination, and transplanting are also important. If the plant came from a cutting, the label will tell when the cutting was made and when rooting took place, also whether rooting hormone was used and what strength. If the plant came from a nursery, this should be noted, with the year purchased; if from a friend add the name of the donor and the date of acquisition. If there was some delay in planting out, add the date.

I hardly ever attempt to put all of these facts on one tiny label, it would be rather like writing the King James Version on a postage stamp. But the facts you omit will invariably be the ones you are asked to provide to the next person you show the plant in question to.

The source of seed or plant is there on all my recent labels, however, and this acts as a trigger for fond memories and idle speculation. And that changes the meaning of the hieroglyphics. Sometimes simple initials of organizations, such as "RHS84," meaning the Royal Horticultural Society, just make me wonder whether I have paid my dues. "NZ" means the Canterbury Alpine Garden Society, and writing it I wonder whether I shall go to New Zealand this year or keep putting it off until I am too old to travel. "BC" brings back last February's winter weekend in Vancouver where I met some of the members of the British Columbia groups including Vera Peck, the seed-exchange director. I saw her garden high on a mountainside with its neat cold frames, a really choice collection of alpines, and a great dog loping around the grounds. Here is a label marked "VP." Not Vera Peck, as you might expect, but Vaclav Plestil, a Czech who collects astragalus. Roxy Gevjan visited him and says he is a tall, thin chain smoker with extraordinary plant knowledge who works for the railway and taught himself English. He sent me seeds of Leguminosae—astragalus and oxytropis and several species of grasses from Europe and Asia. With the name Vaclav, I picture him as one of the two fathers in *The Bartered Bride*, going about the sad business of arranging a marriage.

And this label says "J. Kazbal." He is one of the Czechs we sponsor. It also says "Pirin, Bulgaria." Many of the Czechs go to the mountains of Roumania and Bulgaria to bring back seed. I think of Count Dracula racing down the valley to get into his coffin before sunrise, probably too busy to collect.

Another label says "*Papaver ?alpinum* Jugoslavia MJ83." This plant is a fat round mound with white poppies about six inches high. It was found by Margaret Jordan on holiday. She is the head of a group in South Yorkshire where I was born. At the time I lived there I had no idea some of the best growers in

England lived close by in Dewsbury and Huddersfield. The plant collector E. K. Balls spent his last years close to Margaret's home, and she got to know him and some of his history. I think of her garden with a miniature pool by the gate and one glorious *Sisyrinchium douglasii* growing by it. There was also a tiny glass house with only peach trees in it.

This label says "*Penstemon ellipticus* C. B. Bailey." We visited "Pete" Bailey's garden in Lethbridge, Alberta, on the way to see my Canadian sister in Medicine Hat. We had been to Glacier National Park and gathered some seeds there. They have labels like "Composite? Glacier83." There were very few flowers after Labor Day, and identification was impossible. C. B. Bailey's garden is really a city garden, small and tightly planned. We had cookies and coffee on the lawn. Here is another Penstemon, "H39 80 Meyer APS85." I don't know Mr. Meyer, but he sends seeds of his crosses to the American Penstemon Society seedlist. Some of the plants that result are very good, some ordinary.

One label reads "Something pretty; Olga: E. Ordille 85." Edith Ordille is a West German married to a United States citizen. She visits Czechoslovakia regularly and knows the great growers there, including Olga Duchacova, who exchanges seed with Edith, who exchanges seed with me. Edith visited our garden last year. Olga collected the seed and forgot the name. We got some of Edith's surplus seed. Edith is building a green-house this year. Another complicated label reads "*Dianthus sp. white*; Brian Mathew; nice, Pam Harper." Do you remember Brian Mathew, who visited the United States a couple of years ago? He gave a talk on bulbs and also wrote two excellent books on bulbs. He gave Winifred Bevington a nice dianthus. Winifred Bevington is celebrated by a saxifrage cross named for her, by Joe Elliot, I believe. She goes to Spain every summer with her husband, Harold, to collect seed of Spanish bulbs. She knew Pam Harper in England when Pam had a heather nursery there. Now Pam is a photographer of gardens and plants and has an extensive library of slides for rent and purchase. Pam doesn't like to throw away seed, so I got this dianthus among a batch of less interesting larger plants. Pam likes larger plants. She gardens in Virginia and belongs to The American Rock Garden

Society "because that is where all the best gardeners are."

Many plants in our gardens remind us of an adventure or a friend. Sometimes with a tear. My best aubrieta is a purple double given to me by Carol Sienko of Ithaca, New York, who died recently. I believe it was given to her by Carl Worth, a well-known plantsman who died some years ago. To keep the connection the label reads "*Aubrieta Carol Sienko.*" Do you have labels with any of these names? Dirigo, Millstream, Siskiyou, Eco, Skycleft, Grout Hill? Do you know what they mean?

My hieroglyphics mean more to me than to you. The day may come when I know my plants well enough to dispense with labels. Meanwhile I need their message.

There is still more information you can store on plastic if you buy colored labels. Use a colored label (red?) for plants that need winter protection in the alpine house, and another color (green, say) for bulbs that need to be dug for summer dormancy. For transplanting seedlings you might use orange labels for plants you will give away and pink ones for the seedling sale. Then you could use a blue label for plants you will dig for the show table. I have a lot of experience with forests of white labels, especially in early spring. I cannot in good conscience recommend using too many different color labels in your garden, however. If you cannot see them they lose their purpose, and if you can you wish you couldn't.

Planting Out

I AM STANDING in the garden, a plant in my hand, in a state of indecision. Where shall I plant it?

I have a new raised bed ready for planting. I have just read an article in an Illinois newsletter where Waid Vanderpoel casually throws out that he has many large troughs each devoted to plants from a single geographic region. The Japanese trough, the Western trough, and so on. What elegance! I have decided to reserve my new bed for European plants. I think my plant is from the Caucasus, or is it Armenia? Is the Caucasus part of Europe, or Asia, or would it count as Asia Minor? Shall I go indoors and check the atlas before I plant it? Shall I make sure

it really is from the Caucasus by looking it up in *Hortus* or the
RHS Dictionary? It would mean tracking a bit of garden into
the livingroom, and it would certainly mean washing my hands.
How important is this geographical segregation? Suppose a plant
has a wide range that includes a bit of Asia and a piece of Europe
too, does it have a choice of troughs? Or are we talking about
endemics? Perhaps I had better forget about geography and
think about the plant.

It is a campanula. I think it is a low one. But what if it is like
C. alliariifolia or *C. persicifolia*. It would look ridiculous in a
raised bed with tiny alpines. I eye the perennial border. But
suppose, after all, it is low; then I can't really put it with the
peonies and the daylilies. Shall I go back to the library and look
it up? I look at the name again. *C. betulaefolia*. Suddenly I remember; it is low and rather choice. I move towards a scree
bed. Do campanulas really like scree? This bed is likely to get
really hot sun in the summer; don't all campanulas like a bit of
shade? Maybe on the east side of the raised bed falling in an
ethereal blue waterfall down the cool side of the bed. I chuckle
at my inspiration. No: if I plant it there it will surely grow
towards the sun and therefore into the bed, and I wouldn't get
the waterfall at all. How about a compromise: on the south side
but near something large enough to give it a bit of shade? Oh,
well, there isn't too much room there; I'd better find a place
with more elbow room—after all, most campanulas like to run
around a bit. I cross to another raised bed with a large maple
giving afternoon shade. Now what else is in flower at the same
time as campanulas? Maybe a dianthus would be a good com-
panion. Look, there is a place next to *Dianthus alpinus* 'Joan's
Blood.' But wouldn't that color rather obliterate the campanula?
And what about next year? *D. alpinus* is notoriously short-lived,
and so there might not be a color combination at all. In any
case I see that this *Alyssum saxatile* will need all the space up to
the dianthus before long, and it won't leave much room for my
campanula.

Finally I find a place that looks about right. I look at the
neighbors. Bother, one of them is another campanula. *C. turbinata!* It will never do to have two campanulas next to each

other. First, they will encroach, and, second, there will not be enough contrast. Third—and this clinches it—if one of the labels gets broken I won't know which plant belongs to the remaining label. Better to have one unknown campanula than two campanulas with one label. It is now 11:30, and the sun is getting high, if I don't find a spot quickly it may soon be too hot to plant out, and anyway lunch break is imminent. I wander over to a new bed. No: never put new seedlings into new soil; they invariably winter heave.

I go over to a favorite old bed and find a good general area. I look over the possibilities for a particular spot. I crouch to pull out a Johnny-jump-up, and there's another, and here's a dandelion, for goodness sake. I just did this bed. These weeds grow overnight. Soon I am engrossed in pulling weeds and realize I need my favorite cultivator and a weeder. I return to the barn and get the tools. My hands are soon full of weeds, and I need a bucket to put them in. I go back to the barn to get a bucket and thoughtfully bring back a large can of water ready for the final planting in. I plunge into this weedy area, and before long I am weeding a path while the campanula sits on the garden waiting patiently. On my left is a real mess of dead leaves that need clipping. I go back to the barn, now trudging a little, to get the clippers and return to clip off the old leaves. Underneath the soggy mess I find a saxifrage kicked out by the deer. Enraged, I pick it up and look for a place to replant it. It falls apart in my hands. My feelings are now a weird mixture of grief and greed: I can't replant it, but I can pot it up into at least ten pieces. It will be great to have extra plants for the next plant sale. I put down my tools and return to the greenhouse, holding the saxifrage in both hands and moving, arms outstretched, with almost a slight waddle. I pot up some of the pieces and quickly run out of pots. I look around the greenhouse in vain and find I must go back to the barn and search for more. By now it is lunchtime, and after a quick bowl of soup I get back to potting saxifrage pieces. I water the divisions well, load the pots into a tray, and carry them to a cold frame. All the cold frames are full. These cuttings must have some protection for four or five days at least. I shall have to make room in the cold frame no matter what. I decide to remove a tray of plants and plant them out in the garden; this will give me the necessary space. I take the heavy tray and, now at full waddle, return down the garden looking for places to plant out my twenty plants. On the way I pass a campanula sitting on the garden.

Now what on earth is *that* doing there? How could anybody be so stupid as to leave a little campanula seedling standing in the middle of the garden? Look! It's *Campanula betulaefolia*; one of the best! I must get it in right away. Now where shall I put it?

Making a Raised Bed

W HAT FOLLOWS IS not going to be a recipe so much as a few ideas to pick over if you intend making a raised bed. Start with an outline, rectangular is easiest to handle. If you are making the bed on grass you could dig off the sod or use Roundup to get rid of the grass and weeds inside the rectangle. An alternative would be to lay a heavy layer of newspaper over the area. The walls of the bed ought to be made of material that lasts as long as you want the bed to last. You don't have to think rock or dressed fieldstone or italian marble, though any of these would be great. Logs are perfectly good for a short-lived experiment and will be hospitable to roots as they rot down. Ultimately, though, the whole bed will gradually but gracefully sink into the ground, and you will have a bed more like an old sheep dog than a greyhound. Or we have heard of walls made of newspaper which had a novel swirly look. Concrete blocks are easy-ugly; if you can incorporate them into your landscape, they are the easiest way to get quick results. Has anybody found a way of camouflaging that color?

The lowest layer of rock, or whatever, must be sunk into the ground at least slightly. The stability of the bed depends on the lowest course being firmly in place. The outline is now a shallow raised bed, and you can start filling it. I have used unsorted rocks and stones to provide drainage, but the best reason for using waste material such as this is as filler, to increase the height of the bed without using too much soil or compost. The drainage should be ample in the top layers of the bed, but you don't want to go too far out of your way to obtain fill material. Fill the outline foundation to the top before you put on another course; this gives you a stable base for your next layer of wall. The material that goes on top of the filler should be good soil, the kind you would use in a rock bed. I use compost obtained by stacking sod upside down in piles for a year or so. This is inevitably full of weed seeds and may contain the occasional living root of quack grass. Try to eliminate weed roots as you pile in the soil. As you mix it with sand and peat moss some of the roots will stare you in the face and invite expulsion.

If you can afford it, the next top layer could be a soilless mix such as Jiffymix mixed with coarse sand. This acts as a weed suppressant for the seeds waiting for light in the lower layers. Finally a thick layer of coarse sand, at least three and up to five inches deep, is needed for alpine plants. This sand is the kind usually used for icy roads in winter; it should contain particles up to an eighth of an inch long. You can probably get it at a quarry.

Meanwhile you have been building the walls layer by layer, and the only reason to stop is that the bed is the right height for you. This of course is a major problem. If the bed is under two feet high you can walk on it, but planting and weeding are as backbreaking and finicky as in an ordinary bed on level ground. If it is three feet high you can sit on the side walls, but you have to plant "sidesaddle," and doing so you could twist one of those muscles above the hip with no trouble. Weeding is nice though, and draping the upper torso across the bed gives you a real feeling of being in there.

Higher still, a raised bed suddenly becomes architecture, and there are all kinds of problems related to engineering and aesthetics that intrude. In fact it probably needs an Italian mason to make such a bed properly. But you do end up with plants at eye level or at least navel level. This gives a new perspective to alpine plants that can only be duplicated by visiting high mountains and finding well-placed cliffs, or by raising a container to eye level—not always easy.

AQUILEGIA SAXIMONTANA *is variable in color and size.*
Grow all columbines from wild-collected seed to avoid
unwanted hybrids.

Well, why, then should we bother to make raised beds at all?
The answer is really to do with the plants themselves. Weeds
are under control in a raised bed. The sorrel and dandelions at
ground level cannot climb the wall, and weed seeds tend to
arrive in ones and twos so that eradication is easy. Drainage is
as good as you want to make it. Even a little height sets the
plants off. Air circulation is better higher above the ground.
You can walk around the bed and see plants from several angles.
You may need to water occasionally in droughty weather, though.
In theory the roots go quickly through the sand down to the
rich compost below, and dry weather is not a problem, but in
fact the root system really does expand easily though not always
downward, and many plants will suffer in hot dry weather.

In other words raised beds make just one more way to try
to grow alpine plants. It is only by trial and error (i.e., death)
that you can determine which plants will enjoy a raised bed.
Easy plants will romp in such a bed, and you have to exercise
restraint in the initial planting or you will fill the bed with plants

that don't need such luxury. On the other hand they are easy to remove from sand, and you can practically pull up a hefty lump of thyme with one hand.

There are some plants that seem to hate these rather hungry and thirsty conditions. Saxifrages probably need a shady corner, especially mossies. Androsaces have not done all that well for me in raised beds, except for the annuals and Carnea types. Many will stay alive but without exuberance. Asperulas and many crucifers are fine. My philosophy is to grow plants that like the conditions offered them. In general I avoid watering, but every year there is one protracted period without rain, and an hour with the hose is needed mostly to soothe my nerves. A plant that is really unhappy should be moved somewhere else and not fussed over except when first planted.

The Easiest Art

THIS IS PHOTOGRAPHY, of course. You go into a shop, put down anything from fifteen to fifteen hundred dollars, read the instructions (often translated from the Japanese), load, aim, press the button. Four days later the artwork is returned to you like magic, and you are ready to give a slide talk on growing alpines. The truth is not thus.

Look at the man. He is on his stomach in the dewy grass with his camera pointed towards a saxifrage. He is puffing a little, perhaps it is too soon after breakfast to be assuming such an athletic pose. His neck is thrown back as he peers through the lens. One eye is screwed tight closed giving his face a pained look. His glasses lie on the grass close to his knee, and a minor accident appears imminent. He is adjusting the aperture. The camera is amusingly described as being "on automatic." This means he doesn't need a light meter to determine the F-stop. "The F-stop" is one of the mysterious terms involved in the translation from the Japanese. He twiddles the back ring to get the needles aligned. His neck gives an audible click, then the firmer click of the camera is heard. Suddenly a gasp of irritation: "I forgot to focus!" He rolls over for a little relief from his athletic pose and avoids his glasses but hits a stone with his

DICENTRA CUCULLARIA, *a charming woodlander difficult to photograph.*

kneecap. He rises from prone and assumes kneeling position, leans low, and starts the preparations again. This time he twiddles the ring, gets the F-stop correct, and focuses on the saxifrage. Now he is slightly too high and gets a birdseye view instead of the horizontal aspect he would like. He hunches his shoulders to compensate for the height. His knee hits a small stone, and he returns to prone position with a slight grunt. He must refocus, and now his finger hovers over the button ready to press. A cloud moves over the sun. The aperture must be adjusted, and he again twiddles the ring to get the F-stop correct. He holds his breath and ignores the discomfort of his elbows as his whole body tenses to preserve immobility. Click. Suddenly a screech of anguish: "I forgot to change the ASA!" His last roll of film was ASA 100, and he is now working with ASA 64, a slower film. All his pictures will be overexposed.

Beginners make errors on their way to getting the hang of things. My first camera had a separate view finder; that is, you did not look through the lens of the camera when you used it. I took many a roll of film with the lens cap on. And the wrong ASA number. Eventually I stuck a luggage label on the camera which read, "Check the lens cap. Check the ASA." I graduated to a single-lens reflex camera, so the lens cap stopped being a problem: you couldn't see anything unless you took it off. But I still forgot to change the ASA setting whenever I used a different type of film. I have now moved up to a macro lens. I resisted the move in the face of expert advice from Pam Harper. The reason: camerashopphobia. If you don't know what there is you don't know what to ask for. Do you trust those slick young men in camera shops, all of them pushing the model due to be obsolete by next Christmas?

When it works the macro lens is great. In practice it is *one more thing*, another ring to twiddle and misuse, or forget to use. Photography may be the art most easily reduced to good habits and a good sense of what makes a good picture (I exclude the mysteries of the darkroom), but it is not without its special pains and frustrations.

Why then does one take photographs? Isn't it obvious? You don't *have* a plant until you have a slide of it. No matter how many people see your *Physoplexis comosa*, two years later when the plant is dead, nobody believes you grew it. If you have a slide, not only do they have to believe you grew it, it becomes part of your garden *for all time*. You can show the slide and not mention the length of the plant's brief life. And even if you modestly admit that you no longer have the plant, it is implicit that what you did once you can do again if you really want to. You can then leave the impression that your tastes have changed and that physoplexis is not needed in your present garden design. Alas, dear reader, do not believe everything these slidesmen say. After my own phyteuma perished I tried unsuccessfully each year thereafter to repeat my triumph. The slide remains, a treasure beyond compare.

Gardening Follies

A HISTORY OF gardening usually has something to say about those monuments of conspicuous consumption, the gazebos, grottos, and fake ruins that dotted the parks and large gardens of the nineteenth-century rich. The word "folly" is usually reserved for some observation tower or nonsense structure erected ostensibly to fulfill a brag or celebrate the memory of a spouse, but more likely just to impress. Would the Taj Mahal be included?

There are other follies that more recent, less affluent gardeners have perpetrated. I don't myself know any perpetrators outside of this household, but judging by the catalogs that flood the mails each spring there are plenty of people out there with a good eye and the ready cash for a folly.

Today there was a brief shower, and N. went out to garden wearing a typical ballpark folly—inexpensive, but a true folly nonetheless. This is a small umbrella with alternate green and white panels and a headband, designed to be used as a hat. At first glance it looks like an ideal way to protect oneself from the rain and keep the hands free to weed. After a moment's reflection or a few seconds of experimentation, however, you quickly realize that the slightest breeze would lift the umbrella from your brow, and whatever dignity you had left after putting on this ridiculous device would be lost in retrieving it. This is typical of follies. They look as though they could be useful, decorative, or interesting. We pay for them. We find incontrovertible flaws. We feel, and sometimes look, foolish at having succumbed to their lure.

Take the case of the electric snow shovel which requires plugging into an outdoor outlet often buried in snow and fails to move even a two-inch snowfall. Or the collapsible snow shovel that was meant to be stashed away in the trunk of a car but which fell apart at the slightest resistance. On paper both looked fine.

To return to garden follies, I have a rubber rake, too soft to move leaves from the lawn let alone soil in a bed, but too clumsy to get leaves off a bed in the fall. I remember with regret the beautiful pot shaped like a swan, carried back from Mexico at a great inconvenience that was fired at too low a temperature and melted in the summer rain, spilling soil and rhodohypoxis over the patio. Then there are all the mechanical sprays for fruit trees and weed disposal which clog or jam after half an hour's use, the hose sprays with an optional multitude of stream choices none of which quite work and all of which are accompanied by a steady drip down one's wrist or a maiming jet onto an unsuspecting seedling, the watering cans of wondrous shape with leaky roses. Closer to being a pure folly, and not just poorly designed, is the little gadget that dispenses seed of varying sizes. I assume it has a purpose if you are sowing a row of beets, but I never figured how it could be used to sow packet after packet of alpine seed.

Then there was the cold frame that was supposed to open and close thermostatically. That was a dead loss because getting into the frame was so tiresome and because the first high wind ripped the flexible plastic top. Might work if you live in a cave. Actually most of my cold frames are follyish. I am all thumbs with a saw and hammer, so the ones I have, I had made to my own design specifications, and all have serious flaws. The problem is really lids. They should be light enough not to wrench your shoulder when you raise them, heavy enough so that the wind doesn't send them sailing across the garden, strong enough so that they can be dropped without shattering, rigid enough to bear the weight of a loaded tray, and cheap enough that you can afford them. If you stop to think, there really is no suitable material available.

There are living follies too. Dwarf fruit trees that never bear, dwarf conifers that suddenly transmute into giants, expensive rhododendrons that are half a zone outside their hardiness range, male hollies, bayberries, and the like without a female to give us berries, *Sternbergia lutea*, which won't flower but won't die. Is it the hallmark of a good gardener that he never tries to grow the impossible? I think not. Most of us are ready enough to try *Eritrichium nanum* one more time. Such folly might lead to triumph and fame. Yet the Shakers had an edict against wasting time growing plants not hardy in Massachusetts.

Our latest folly is a weeding wagon which consists of a tractor seat mounted on two wheels low enough to sit on and weed as you roll. Unfortunately it is too heavy to carry to the bed you want to weed and is not arranged for riding any great distance as it lacks steering mechanism and power. Oh, well, I guess it will hang in the barn with the old-fashioned push cultivator, the fancy hoes, and the machete. Meanwhile I sometimes feel the whole garden is a folly. But at least it isn't a monument to a dearly beloved, nor is its reason for existence to win a bet. The garden's one purpose is to be a source of immense satisfaction, especially when the griefs of last spring are past and forgotten and the hopes of next spring have not yet matured. And it is "a poor thing but mine own."

The Zone Game

D O   Y O U   P L A Y the zone game when you go on a car trip? One March day we drove from the Berkshires to Stamford in the southwest of Connecticut, about a hundred miles south. We started off from home at 1,400 feet above sea level in Zone 1 with three of four inches of snow covering the entire garden and patches of ice where recent rains had fallen and frozen. Although it was mid-March there wasn't a rustle of spring within earshot despite steady rain the day before. We drove down Norfolk Road, half a mile of unpaved dirt, now treacherous with frozen ruts, to get on to the hard-top to Colebrook. By the time we hit Colebrook, seven miles south, there were patches of earth and grass showing through the snow—Zone 2. We descended the hill into Winsted and took Route 8 to Torrington and Waterbury. By now there were patches of snow lying on bare earth. Zone 3, winter at its ugliest. There were remnants of its beauty on the man-made cliffs blasted out of the hillside when the highway was made, where a gigantic icefall draped the rocks. South of Waterbury the snow had disappeared completely, the trees looked fresh washed by the recent rain, and we finally saw flowers on some of the trees. Zone 4. By the time we hit the parkway going east to Stamford there was grass growing on the verges and pale yellow flowers of witch hazel in a backyard. Zone 5!

We checked the zones on the return trip. They really exist. Each region had a character that was recognizably distinct from the others. Of course, this is March when differences are at their most obvious, but you can see them at other times too. A map of North America showing hardiness zones shows the country divided into a series of regions according to average minimum winter temperature. The region we passed through on this short trip is in Zones 5 and 6 according to most maps. At this time of year the differences from north to south are startling. Being 1,400 feet above sea level suddenly becomes significant too, comparable to being above the snow line on a real mountain. The crude divisions on the national map pay no attention to the subtleties of altitude.

These ephemeral and comparatively small climatic distinctions give a strong local flavor to gardening, especially in spring and fall. Gardens near Long Island Sound can be alive with crocuses and snowdrops while Berkshire gardens are icebound. "They" can dig; we can only fret and complain. Why does anybody live north of Long Island? (Or Virginia, or Florida?) Well, when spring finally does come, the North has a glory comparable to its fall display. Snowdrops, daffodils, and tulips all bloom together. The drabas have hardly finished before the alyssums and *Phlox subulatas* begin. The New England spring is short but intense. If you live south of Long Island spring is over by mid-May. What a pity.

My own garden is full of zones, too. I put snowfence up each November to slow down the snow so that it accumulates on the leeward side. I place the fence so that snow falls on a bed I want to protect. This means there are areas of the garden where the snow, being thicker, lingers longer. There are areas where the snowmelt forms wet patches, even two-day streams and six-day ponds, where plants are under water and ice for long stretches of time. Other areas are raked by the January blasts and can lose their snow cover the day after a storm. What zone are they in? Surely a different climate from the plants that remain under deep snow for much longer. The average minimum winter temperature is an inadequate description of the climate of a garden. We have to read our official zone number as an average for a large region. Our own garden may be up to one zone higher or lower than the average, and parts of our garden may be a zone higher or lower still. If you live in Zone 5, there may be parts of your garden which are the equivalent of Zone 7, and on the other hand there may be parts which have a climate like Zone 3. I haven't studied the calibration of zonery sufficiently; it may well be that a spread of three zone units could be found in a single garden. This is very exciting because it opens up the possibility of growing a greater range of plants. The wide local variation in zone effects, at any rate, certainly gives you confidence to try new plants and removes the oppressive strictures of the bible thumpers who want you to know you are wasting time. You might even be able to turn around and say "Oh, but I can grow *Rhododendron pemakoense* in northwest Albany"—or wherever. Of course you have to face the prospect of losing face when next winter brings no snow to that part of the garden, with abnormally low temperatures and a January thaw that acts like an internal alarm clock on the wretched rhododendron, waking it up in time for a February freeze. Next May you find the bark has split and you write off another plant as irredeemably tender. Well, if you had it for five years you shouldn't complain too much. Nothing is forever, and anyway, if a plant looks like outlasting you it will gradually assume more importance to your friends than you yourself have. Do you want people to say, "There's that wonderful *Rhododendron pemakoense* growing in northwest Albany. So old! It used to belong to old so-and-so. . . . I forget his name. What a wonderful plant!" Never "what a remarkable gardener old so-and-so was."

So play the zone game in your garden. Take note of those parts of the garden that qualify as high-zone areas. You may then be able to order with confidence the plants in the catalogs described as "for a south-facing wall" or "protect in winter." Also note the areas that seem to come out of winter with most of the plants windburned, frost heaved, or completely dead. Cherish the plants that do survive, and give them leave to stay a while and multiply.

Phyllotaxis

FRESHMAN MATH STUDENTS get a kick out of infinite sequences, for instance, the sequence 1,3,5,7, etc. consists of the odd numbers, and the next term is obviously 9. A standard problem is to ask what is the next term of the sequence when a certain number of terms is given. One trick sequence is 4,14,23,28,34,42, . . . The next term here is 50, as these are the local stops on the subway on Manhattan's West Side. You could also baffle a mathematician/rock gardener with the following trick sequence: *Uvullaria, Carex, Malus, Plantago,* . . . What is the next term? The answer turns out to be *Sempervivum*, and you may be interested in the explanation, which links botany, mathematics, and art.

Some plants have their leaves in opposite pairs on the stem. In some other plants the leaves are arranged in a pattern called "alternate." This technical term means that the leaves appear singly along the stem. Also alternate leaves are never in a single row one immediately above the other. Instead the second leaf up will sometimes be on exactly the opposite side of the stem, that is, half a revolution from the first leaf. If this happens to be the case then all the successive leaves are placed 180 degrees from the previous leaf. The third leaf is thus immediately above

the first leaf, the fifth leaf is above the third, and so on. Sometimes the second leaf is placed at one third of a revolution from
the first, and the third leaf is one third of a revolution from the
second. This means the fourth leaf will be immediately above
the first. The angle of rotation is the same for all the leaves on
the plant. Moreover, it is the same for all the plants of that
species, and more mysterious still, it is the same for all the
members of that genus. Notice that the angle of rotation could
be thought of as two thirds of a revolution in the opposite
direction. In any case, either fraction—⅓ or ⅔—describes the
amount of the turning to get to the next leaf on the stem. Are
you amazed? Well, I now have to recant a little. You know how
careless Nature can be: none of her circles is quite true, the
spheres bulge, if it's supposed to be five it is sometimes six, if
it's sexangular you can only count five, and so on. Just as you
thought you had pinned down a description of a plant you find
something which doesn't quite fit. You try another specimen,
and that doesn't fit either. In fact you come to the conclusion
that the only true plants are the ones in botanical illustrations.
All the plants we find are mutilated, sick, or mutants if we
believe the description. But if you allow for accidents of growth
and a little fudging around the edges by Mrs. Nature you can
get some of the flavor of what it would be like to be both a
mathematician and god. Back to our incomplete series of plants.

First the genus *Uvullaria*. These plants have one leaf every
half revolution. The third leaf up is directly above the first; the
second leaf is 180 degrees or ½-revolution from the first (in
either direction). We will associate the fraction ½ with *Uvullaria*.

Next *Carex*: In this case the fourth leaf is directly above the
first. Successive leaves are ⅓ of a revolution from each other,
⅔ if you go the opposite direction. We will associate either
fraction—⅓ or ⅔—with *Carex*.

In the case of genus *Malus* the sixth leaf is above the first.
This means that the leaves are separated by an angle which is
a multiple of ⅕ of a revolution. It is in fact ⅖ of a revolution,
or ⅗ if you go in the other direction—never ⅕ or ⅘.

The next fraction belongs to *Plantago*. This is ⅜. The ninth
leaf is above the first. The angle of rotation could also be ⅝ in

the opposite direction. So we have a sequence of fractions corresponding to our plant groups: ½, ⅔, ⅗, ⅝, . . . I have used the larger fraction in each case.

Notice how each fraction is constructed; the next numerator is the denominator of the previous fraction, and the new denominator is obtained by adding the numerator and denominator of the previous fraction. The next fraction so constructed would be ⁸⁄₁₃, and then ¹³⁄₂₁, and so on. These numerators are the consecutive terms of the sequence: 1,1,2,3,5,8,13,21,34,55, . . . This particular series is called the Fibonacci sequence after a thirteenth-century Italian mathematician whose real name was Leonardo of Pisa.

We can now read the fraction ⅝ as saying that we require 5 revolutions of the stem to get 8 leaves. All the leaves are ⅝ of a revolution (225 degrees) apart, or, going in the reverse direction, ⅜-revolution (135 degrees). What plant's leaf-position fraction follows *Plantago*? That of Genus *Sempervivum* has the fraction ⁸⁄₁₃. If you want to go any higher you have to look at pine cones.

All the genera with alternate leaves appear to fit one or another of these patterns. If you hold an actual flower stem in your hand you will be lucky to identify the pattern right away. A good time to look at trees if you want to see their leaf arrangements is in the winter when the buds are clearly visible. If you are pulling off the leaves of a semp, poor thing, you could be disappointed.

An added fillip to this most mysterious state of affairs is the extension into art. If the sequence of fractions yielding the Fibonacci series is extended indefinitely, the fraction approaches a definite number called the Golden Section. Aesthetically this ratio describes the rectangle thought to have the most harmonious dimensions. The fraction's exact value is given by the formula $(\sqrt{5} + 1) \div 2$, which is about 1.618. The reciprocal of this magic number is .618. If you cut off a square side 1 from a rectangle with sides 1.618 and 1, you are left with a rectangle sides 1 and .618, which has exactly the same proportions as the original rectangle. Rectangles of these relative dimensions were used by many Renaissance painters and architects.

I don't think modern botanists have much time for such romantic theories, and since no satisfactory explanation of the harmoniousness of the Golden Section has been given, we are left in the realm of mysticism. You could probably extract some cogent arguments out of it for the existence or non-existence of God.

I once asked a geologist if he thought mountains were beautiful. His reply indicated that knowing how they were formed actually increased his enjoyment of their beauty. The same may be true of botany; instead of reducing our loved ones to specimens and statistics, maybe more intellectual curiosity and a more informed look at plants would increase our fun. Phyllotaxis, the arrangement of leaves on a stem, could be a gentle start to putting this curiosity into practice. I can't promise to try it out until at least July, though, I'll be much too busy until then.

Gardens to Admire

I WISH I COULD have called this piece "Great Gardens," but the connotation would be wrong. If a garden is called "great," you expect that to be the consensus of the gardening world at least, and of the coffee-table-book-reading public in particular. You expect the garden to be the product of a certain amount of "history" and a good deal of money. You expect landscape à la Capability Brown or at least *allées* and avenues, fountains and statuary. You expect a centerpiece of a palace, a mansion, or an abbey, a house that earns its title of Residence. Failing a Residence, there had better be at least the ruins of one.

But so often this type of great garden is short on interesting plant material. It may excel in ancient trees and shrubby plants; it may even have a good perennial border, an arboretum, or acres of glass. Very, very rarely, however, does it have really interesting rock-garden plants. So I want to mention a few gardens I think are great in a different sense. I feel free to bypass Wisley, Kew, and other great botanical gardens because they are really conglomerates, encyclopedias instead of books, and the parts that are really interesting to me are only a detail of the grand whole. In fact none of my own "great gardens" are public gardens in any sense, and you can't visit them unless you have ingratiated yourself with the owner and found a mutually agreeable time to visit. Besides I'm not going to tell you the phone numbers or addresses, and rather than encourage you to visit I shall say please don't. This would be quite contrary, however, to the spirit of the American Rock Garden Society, whose members on the whole like visitors and do in fact make strangers welcome.

In order to have convenient pigeonholes in which to classify these gardens, I will ignore geography and conjure up a kind of local sociology rather than history, and a more modest time frame than those of Blenheim or Longwood.

First, then, consider the garden in a country town or made around a suburban house. Sometimes a garden has already been established before the current owner takes over, and no major changes are considered necessary. I think of my sister Margaret's garden in Yorkshire, England: pleasant enough when taken over, but now, with more serious attention given to plant material, its interest grows each year. This garden has its own personality with odd bits of the ancient local parish church scattered around. Weather worn or storm damaged and discarded, they have had their original place usurped by unlovely twentieth-century replicas. A patio more or less surrounds the house with plants growing in the paving, and a raised bed is established under mature trees where rock plants grow without interference from tree roots. The rest of the garden is a perennial border framed by a boundary fence with almost full grown trees for shade and protection. Margaret doesn't think of it as a Great Garden, but it is an illustration of the difference a fresh eye can bring to an old garden. I had a similar situation in Hempstead, Long Island. I poured my love and money into decorating a suburban azalea garden with species crocus, tulips, narcissus, erythroniums, and other bulbs that bloomed from October through mid-May. I never thought of the garden as really mine once the azaleas started, and I left the house for other places, returning in September to plant more bulbs.

A garden near Boston made by Bob and Joan Means on

hungry gravel is a good example of what can be done with an unpromising site. The effect is partially achieved by an extremely realistic but fake stream recirculating its water and running just about the length of the garden. I imagine water has to be fed into the stream too; the plants growing along the stream must use up quite a bit of moisture. These include *Cypripedium reginae* and other treasures. The "source" of the stream is close to the house and camouflaged by rock work. Most of the rest of the ornamental part of the garden consists of rock plants. The non-ornamental part includes vegetables and a place for livestock very neatly incorporated into the picture.

Jean Everett in central Connecticut has a pond which is either natural or an enhanced hollow in a low part of the grounds. The hollow is surrounded by wet-loving iris and grasses. But it isn't the focal point of the garden. This is a sunken area closer to the house, giving the effect of a shallow quarry adorned with raised beds and containers filled with pretty mats and buns. The garden has no edges and seems to merge into the woods on one side and drift into a vegetable garden and ultimately an astonishing Christmas-tree farm on the other. The pond, which makes such an impression when you arrive, is finally almost a mere appendage to the central area.

There is a garden in Seattle by Betty Lowry which is as close to perfection as you can get in a garden with definite boundaries. This consists mostly of raised beds with rocky outcrops, and the plants are choice, beautifully grown, and substantial. Harold and Winnie Bevington's garden in Surrey, England, is also a jewel box. Both gardens are in favored climates with plenty of interest all through the year. Harold is a rock-garden evangelist. One of his selling points is the notion of a year-round activity. So it is for them in Surrey; I have to leave my garden for three winter months but still think it worthwhile.

Ev. Whittemore's Massachusetts garden is no more, but it's well worth mentioning. After a swimming pool had outlived its usefulness, it was removed. In its place several tons of basalt were dumped one day as Ev. took a rake and pushed and pulled the dark-grey rock into miniature mountains and valleys. This became the core of a fascinating garden with high alpines growing in the basalt, a bog in one of the hollows, and down one side of the garden a fake stream trickling through a fine collection of orchids and woodlanders. Ev.'s ideas (and plants) have now been translated to a North Carolina mountain. Here the stream is real, and the basalt has been replaced by local stone of various sizes. The result is the spitting image of the top of Independence Pass, in the Colorado Rockies. We are waiting for a report from Ev. on what will survive the muggy summers of North Carolina. This garden is high and may represent a new experiment in that region. When you think of Ev.'s garden you have to remember Ron Beckwith's basalt slopes. I don't know which garden came first, but the growing conditions are similar even if the effect is different. Ev.'s garden was surrounded by tall trees, while Ron's is open to full sun. I haven't seen its recent development, but there were superb alpines reveling in the top-of-the-Rockies environment.

Many gardens are dominated by a natural feature or a man-made one. Two of the most spectacular are built on rocky outcrops of gigantic size. Margot Parrot's rock, north of Boston, is a sheer cliff less than six feet from the back door of the house. The rock rises abruptly, receding gradually at bedroom-window level and more rapidly at higher elevations. Pockets of good soil have been prepared in the rock face and good alpines planted in this naturalistic setting. Much of the work required extreme care and agility, and for some spots, ropes and ladders. It is far too dangerous to allow casual visitors to clamber around the rock, but the effect from the ground is stunning. The other great rock belongs to Harriet Sornberger in northeast Connecticut. It is a good fifty yards from the house and separated from the lovely perennial and herb gardens around the house by a stone wall. A green sward leads up to it, and the rock was stripped of weeds and weed trees before being garlanded with a mountain track and planted with dwarf conifers and alpines.

Close by the Parrot garden is Catherine Hull's magnificent rock garden. The property is at the summit of a steep hill, and there is a wild garden sloping down from the house with great views of distant ocean. But the feature that epitomizes the garden is a tufa wall with large beds of rock plants. These include all of the standards but also many of the most treasured rock plants in the repertory. Separating rock gardens from the wild cliff is extensive stonework consisting of walls, steps, fountains, and an entertaining life-size statue of Neptune looking out to sea.

Kris Fenderson's barn is the dominant feature of his beautifully landscaped garden. There is a natural stream flowing through the garden, which has been tamed enough to house a mass planting of primulas. *Primula japonica* and *P. bulleyana* grow there, as well as some of the larger species you don't often see— *P. florindae* and even *P. flaccida*. Above the primulas is a cage bridging the water where a family of ducks hangs out, and as you walk up the stream you may encounter a couple of Highland cattle behind an electric fence. But all this is, so to speak, "behind" the barn. The main drag is a terraced lawn with gorgeous perennial island beds. The Fenderson property is in New Hampshire at a highish elevation, so coming across this opulent spread is a real surprise. As you stand among the delphiniums and phlox and look down towards an open field, you realize that the meadow is an arboretum of dwarf conifers. Close to the main garden the conifers are grouped in beds, and many are weeping or contorted forms with the characteristic look of maimed birds. A public unpaved road runs between the garden and the ancient house, enhancing the garden's feeling of aloofness and dignity.

In Dick and Herbert Redfield's garden in Scotland, Connecticut, the stream is a magnet even though it isn't central to the site. In fact it is hidden by trees, and the paths that lead you by stony beds of cactus drive you inexorably towards the streamside and the woodland garden that borders it. By the stream the Candelabra primulas are glorious. Sydney Eddison in Newtown, Connecticut also has a primrose garden planted around a stream that barely struggles through the summer but keeps the soil damp enough to support primulas of the Vernales section: *P. vulgaris, P. elatior. P. X juliana*. This is almost a secret garden that is separated from the perennials by a wall with a gate that leads you into the holy of holies.

Mary Ley also in the Newtown area has a construction of

huge rocks to work with. Water trickles into pools Japanese fashion, and the stylish rock formations with mountain tracks are swathed with thymes and great mats of *Silene acaulis*. This garden required a bulldozer and an eminent landscaper, Karl Grieshaber, to put it in place. The Harveys in Woodstock, Connecticut, used another designer-contractor, Howard Pfeifer, to lay gargantuan rocks in artistic juxtaposition with ingeniously piped water and comfortable promenading and viewing platforms. This is a recent construction and needs time to mellow. Howard Pfeifer's own garden is essentially a rhododendron garden, but the focal point is a rock garden built around a pool very close to the house. There is a very intimate feeling about the garden in spite of an *allée* of laburnum leading to it. The trees and shrubs act as protectors of the central patio.

Nick Nickou's southern-Connecticut garden spreads out around the house in all directions and divides itself into regions but not rooms. There are secret places here and there but also an open quality as though everything led naturally to everything else. The great emphasis here is on rare and beautiful woody plants, and the effort has been helped by the fact that the garden has a comparatively gentle climate. A garden tour becomes a worshipful pilgrimage from tree to unexpected tree. The beds of alpines play a secondary role.

Another unusual garden in Newtown is Jim York's. At car-entering level dry walls and raised beds planted with alpines border the driveway. At the same level through the living room and at the rear of the house is a platform overlooking a steep hillside garden with a strong Italian flavor. It is not by any means formal, though. Winding paths descend through a large area planted with perennials and clipped dwarf conifers and, of course, no grass until the bottom of the hill is reached. By that time the grass no longer needs to pretend to be lawn, and the garden merges into the nearby woods and meadows. A stream trickles down the hillside, adding atmosphere but not asserting a strong presence. You can find hostas here in great variety and some whimsical topiary.

Some gardens are dominated even more by their site, especially if the site is very steep. One such garden is in North

Vancouver, where Daphne Guernsey has transformed an almost sheer hillside between two mountain roads into a garden with paths and steps bordered by shrubs and beds hugging the slopes for dear life. There is hardly enough elbow room to walk, let alone work, but the feeling is invigorating and exciting. Another garden with a position almost as sheer is on a fell side in England's Lake District. Dilys Davies has carved a fantasy garden out of the mountain turf there. The house is half a mile along a dirt road which has a gradient of 1 in 3 part of the way; the road suddenly drops fifty or a hundred feet into the backyard of the house. The garden continues the downward sweep below the house, and there are dizzying views of the valley if you can spare the time to look away from the garden. The planting is a closely packed mix of shrubs and perennials with rock plants not necessarily segregated. The main paths are either terraces or steep, and the working paths are hair-raising. Everybody likes to give names to different sections of their own gardens, if only as reference points. In this garden you get the "Himalayas" and "Thermopylae."

Judy Glattstein's garden in southern Connecticut is dominated by the remnants of a graceful wood. There is a rock scree above the house, but the business part of the garden is below the house where a wood-chip path wanders among stands of Japanese arisaemas, trilliums, sanguinarias, and many of the better plants of the Eastern United States. On a larger scale is a Massachusetts garden belonging to Sam and Beverly Rayburn. This is also a woodland garden with cypripediums and trilliums in May and a great collection of hollies. There is a massive rocky outcrop closer to the house which is enlivened with pools and running water and Japanese bridge. But beautiful as the rocks and water are, it is the woodland down below them which draws the eye and invites a stroll. Woodland gardens always give the impression of low maintenance, but against that are the fun and work of clearing the jungle in the first place and later laying the paths and beds. These have to give the appearance of naturalness, though the surrounding forest denies the very notion.

Linc and Timmy Foster's Millstream garden in northwestern Connecticut is the "natural" garden par excellence. The house and arrival point are at the bottom of a mountain, and the garden occupies several acres of the mountainside. Closest to the house is a collection of alpines in raised beds, containers, patios, and walls. You could spend hours here and not realize that this was not the whole garden. In fact while vastly interesting it is almost an insignificant part of the whole. So leave the saxifrages and ramondas and climb upwards through the alpine lawn. This is a chameleon garden. In May you think the garden is all phlox, in June you change your mind and see geraniums everywhere. There are "no" weeds; all the plants run into each other, acting out the role of weeds when they are not in bloom but shining out center stage when it is their turn. The culmination of the alpine lawn is a mat of *Daphne cneorum* yards across, which incredibly is a single plant. As you examine the alpine lawn at Millstream, you are conscious of a lot of water noise, and you finally see the mountain torrent which gives the garden its name. It is a feature to be reckoned with; the noise can be deafening, the visual effect magnificent. But the stream has a life of its own which permits only a limited degree of taming. Some of the splashier areas make a great home for primulas.

A bridge crosses the stream, and a path leads up into the woods. You suddenly realize that this after all is the garden, the open part down below is just hors d'oeuvre for the main rhododendron garden. If it were only rhododendrons it would be beautiful, true, but interesting mostly to another specialist. As it is, the understory of the shrubs and trees is a collection of woodland plants such as you have never encountered before. Phlox, arisaemas, ericaceous plants, ferns, shortias—you can find scores of species. Sun lovers are growing in clearings and seem to be grown as specimens for the fun of it. Shade tolerant plants are in their element and form vigorous colonies. *Phlox buckleyi* and *P. adsurgens; Arisaema sikokianum* and other rare aroids. The soil is midway between forest duff and sandy loam. By this time we are some distance from the house, and the stream is out of sight in a rather steep canyon. How do they water? Well, they don't! It seems the rain falls on days they plan to plant out, so they don't really need to water. When you have climbed the woodland path until you are certain you must have reached the end of the garden you find great beds of rhododendron seedlings and raised beds of interesting alpines. One rock is a cradle for *Lewisia cotyledon* forms in orange, pink, and white.

The descent path goes close to a rock overlooking the ravine, and one looks down on a sea of azaleas. The impression is that of a steep Himalayan valley with a mountain stream rushing through. Heaven with no leeches.

Phil Cook's Vermont garden is still young but different from most others in idea. Well, you can see the same idea in Eloise Lesan's garden with its exposed rock ledge. The latter is in southern Connecticut. Eloise has planted pockets in the ledge where it descends the hillside overlooking the water at Cos Cob. On the exposed rock at the top sits the house. In front of it a part of the rock is hollowed out to form a shallow pool for birds to splash in. Phil's garden has the same heroic dimensions as Linc Foster's, but the interest is in exposed rock with pockets of soil planted with alpines. The garden is so vast that the cultivated part is indistinguishable from the mountainside until you are amongst the rocks. There are plenty of interesting trees placed strategically, not forming the dense groves of Linc's rhododendrons. It may be a difference in maturity or simply a difference in style.

Is Fred Watson's garden dominated by the site? Probably, although it is the most assisted site of any I have seen. Perched on a hill in New Hampshire, the garden around the house is engulfed in stonework used for walls, walks, patios, and rock beds, all expertly laid and beautiful to behold. The "feature" of the garden is the winter protection offered to Fred's cherished New Zealand plants, and to any other treasure that thinks it needs coddling. This protection is a collection of walk-in "cold frames" erected over some of the beds in October and pretty well wind proofed. Some of them have underground heating cables. The plants love it. They certainly prefer this treatment to being dug and stored in a greenhouse. Beyond the house is a large field/lawn edged by flower beds, shrubs, and wildflowers. In the far corner of the field a large pond provides a home for Asiatic gentians, *Diapensia lapponica*, and other rarities. More movable pavilions protect some of the primulas and anything else that can sneak under cover. All the superstructure is possible because Fred runs a strawberry farm; this ensures having strong arms to do the carting, erecting, and dismantling of these imposing structures when the work on the strawberry beds is at a low ebb.

Back in Connecticut, Ellie and Joel Spingarn have just completed a deer-proof fence. Fortunately it does not dominate the scene. Ellie's stonework is the star here. Her splendid massive walls are planted with alpines of every kind, including daphnes. A great gash of a canyonlike stream divides the garden into two parts. The part that includes the house is essentially two very large rock gardens, again with extensive stonework. The area beyond the stream is a work area and represents the Spingarns' colonizing spirit. But colonization doesn't mean a swiftly made garden, dug and planted in a session. It means new walls planted as they are being built, slowly and carefully. It means work buildings with plumbing and propagation facilities.

But this list has gone on long enough. It could never be complete. Obvious omissions are Harland Hand's California fantasy, the Siskiyou nursery garden, which will be one of the greats in a couple of years, the McGourty perennial garden, and Ted Childs's impressive rock face in Norfolk, Connecticut, Roxy Gevjan's Philadelphia conifer garden, Francisca Dart's arboretum in British Columbia, Ed Leimseider's Japanese and American garden in Westport, Connecticut, John Bieber's little gem on Long Island, Roy Davidson's watery Seattle landscape, and many others.

Hymns of praise are usually sung to the wrong people. I suppose Miss Willmott and the others were great gardeners, but they really had a lot of help. The gardens I love are the brainchildren and the brawnchildren of their owners.

Bibliography

IF A GARDENER asks, "What books should I read?" the only truthful answer is, "Everything." No one person can be plant collector, propagator, landscape designer, historian, hybridist, and botanist all the time; and yet we *are* all these at one time or another, and some great gardeners have managed to be outstanding in many of these activities throughout their lives. It follows that even if there are gardeners who know a lot about a lot of things, nobody knows everything about all aspects of gardening. We have to read books if we want to grasp the broad outlines and then the subtleties of our subject. So here is a list, aimed at rock gardeners primarily, of the books I admire and use most. It is very personal and not meant to be exhaustive or definitive.

There are several categories of gardening books, and some books fall into more than one:

1. *Garden construction.* How to start a garden and how to change the one you have.
2. *What to grow.* Which plants are in cultivation, which are recommended, and where to get them.
3. *Botany and taxonomy.* How to identify a plant by its parts and find a valid name for it.
4. *Plants in the wild.* We want to know which plants grow in a particular location, and we want to know the useful members of a particular genus.
5. *Exploration.* It gives your plants cachet if you can tell a story about their discovery and provenance.
6. *History of gardens*, foreign gardens, famous gardens. In these books we find models for our gardens and get a sense of the continuity of horticulture in time, space, and ideology.
7. *Anecdotal*, literary, and inspirational writing.
8. *Horticulture.* Advice drawn from other people's experiments and experience. Sometimes secondhand and not always sound.

At the top of the list of books for rock gardeners are the journals of the great international societies and some of the more enterprising smaller groups. These journals cover all the above categories at one time or another and after years of collecting issues, you own a genuine reference library. You cannot expect to find an arbitrary subject discussed in the latest issue of a journal, of course; treat them as your quarterly required reading.

The Bulletin of the Alpine Garden Club of British Columbia, 13751 56A Avenue, Surrey, British Columbia V3W 1J4, Canada.
The Bulletin of the Alpine Garden Society, Lye End Link, St. John's, Woking GU21 1SW, England.
The Bulletin of the American Rock Garden Society, 15 Fairmead Road, Darien, Connecticut 06820.
The Bulletin of the Canterbury Alpine Garden Society, 328 Greers Road, Christchurch 5, New Zealand.
The Journal of the Royal Horticultural Society, 80 Vincent Square, London SW1P 2PE, England.
The Journal of the Scottish Rock Garden Club, 21 Merchiston Park, Edinburgh EH10 4PW, Scotland.

To be more sure of finding what we are looking for we refer to encyclopedic works:
The Royal Horticultural Society Dictionary of Gardening. (Oxford: Oxford University Press, 1965). The *RHS Dictionary* is excellent. Its plant names are reliable but not necessarily up-to-date. It has abundant plant references; at first you think all the plants of the world must be included, but later you realize how inadequate any affordable encyclopedic work has to be. The *RHS Dictionary* has much terse horticultural advice more suited to British gardens than those in the United States. Historical and botanical notes add to the enjoyment of browsing. In fact you could extract the elements of botany and taxonomy by piecing together scattered bits of information. Line drawings are usually of plants of no interest to a rock gardener. There is no color, no humor. The four volumes make looking things up sometimes a nuisance. Highly recommended plants are given a star.
Hortus Third (New York: Macmillan, 1978), is a one-volume United States version of the *RHS Dictionary*. It has the advantage of being easier to use, though you need table space to consult

it. I use both reference books equally, and I find there is often confirmation, occasionally a contradiction, and sometimes an "exclusive." *Hortus* is better on American material and sometimes gives hardiness-zone ratings. There are no plant recommendations in *Hortus*, and the drawings are strictly botanical. If you want something more detailed and more technical, you have to go to a flora.

There are many excellent and less expensive gardening encyclopedias such as Taylor, and I would not select any one of them as being vastly superior to the others.

Most of the books on rock gardening follow a typical format. The first part of the book tells you how to make a rock garden, bog garden, raised bed, alpine lawn, container garden, or the like, and gives some general cultural information. Then follows a plant list usually arranged alphabetically, with descriptions and occasionally more specific hints on culture. This organization works well; inclusion in the list is regarded as recommendation for a plant, so no hyperbole is needed in the descriptions. If the author steps out of character and praises a plant it is probably worthwhile pricking your ears over the hint, and if a plant is even slightly damned you had better watch out.

The grandpapa of all these is Reginald Farrer's *The English Rock Garden* reprinted by Theophrastus (Little Compton, Rhode Island: Theophrastus, 1975). The text is overwritten, in decorative, witty prose that makes some people grit their teeth, but it contains so much information you have to forgive some of the idiotic excesses. Sampson Clay continued Farrer's work in *The Present-Day Rock Garden* (Little Compton, Rhode Island: Theophrastus, 1976), but he includes so many unavailable and ungrowable plants that one seldom opens it except to browse and sigh.

Anna Griffith's *Collins Guide to Alpines* (London: William Collins, 1964) fits the standard format and has a useful set of colored pictures that are elderly sirens, still seductive after a quarter of a century. Many gardeners have had it as their aim to grow every plant illustrated in this book.

Rock Gardening by H. Lincoln Foster (Portland, Oregon: Timber Press, 1982) is even better on garden construction and has many more American plants in its lists. This is the bible of every rock gardener in the northeastern states.

Graham Stuart Thomas has written a book, *Perennial Garden Plants* (London: Dent, 1976) which is a classic for perennial gardeners but also very useful for others, and which includes several plants that could be used appropriately in a rock garden.

Other writers have given rock gardeners excellent general reading, for instance George Schenk (for West Coast gardeners), William Schacht, Royton Heath, and Will Ingwersen.

There are a number of books written about SINGLE GENERA:

Androsaces by G. S. Smith and D. D. Lowe (Woking, UK: Alpine Garden Society, 1977)

Asiatic Primulas by Roy Green (Woking, UK: Alpine Garden Society, 1976)

Campanulas by H. Clifford Crook (Little Compton, Rhode Island: Theophrastus, 1977)

Handbook of Garden Iris by William R. Dykes (Little Compton, Massachusetts: Theophrastus, 1976)

The Iris by Brian Mathew (London: Batsford, 1981)

Primulas of Europe and America by Smith, Burrow, and Lowe (Woking, UK: Alpine Garden Society 1984)

Saxifrages and related genera by Fritz Koehlen (Portland, Oregon: Timber Press, 1986)

And some good books on BULBS:

Bulbs of Europe by Christopher Grey-Wilson and Brian Mathew (Lexington, Massachusetts: Stephen Greene Press, 1981)

The Bulb Book by Martin Rix and Roger Phillips (London: Pan, 1984)

The Complete Guide to Bulbs by Patrick M. Synge (New York: Dutton, 1962).

Dwarf Bulbs by Brian Mathew (London: Batsford, 1973)

I don't know of any good book on bulbs written by an American.

Books that concentrate on plants from one geographical location are useful for horticultural purposes and for planning
plant-hunting expeditions:

The Audubon Field Guides to North American Wildflowers (New
York: Knopf, 1979)

Flowers of Greece and the Aegean by Anthony Huxley and William
Taylor (London: Chatto & Windus, 1977)

Flowers of the Himalaya by Oleg Polunin and J.D.A. Stainton
(Oxford: Oxford University Press, 1984)

Flowers of Southwest Europe by Oleg Polunin and B. E. Smythie
(Oxford: Oxford University Press, 1973)

Jewels of the Plains by Claude A. Barr (Minneapolis: University
of Minnesota Press, 1983)

Mountain Flower Holidays in Europe by Lionel Bacon (Woking,
UK: Alpine Garden Society, 1977)

New Zealand Alpine Plants by A. F. Mark and Nancy Adam
(London: A. H. & A. W. Reed Ltd., 1979)

Rocky Mountain Alpines, Jean Williams, editor (Portland, Oregon: Timber Press, 1986)

Wildflowers of the Pacific Northwest by Lewis Clark (Sidney, British Columbia: Gray's Publishing Ltd., 1976)

There are also plenty of travel books from the early twentieth
century relevant to gardening. The mixture of familiar plants
and obsolete attitudes makes for exasperating reading and will
appeal to historically minded gardeners.

I use two textbooks. You can get a copy of Gray's *Manual
of Botany* at a secondhand bookshop in a university town. Read,
too, *Botanical Latin* by William T. Stearn (Newton Abbot, UK:
David and Charles, 1985). This is easy reading if you have had
a couple of years of Latin and helps with the understanding and
remembering of plant names.

Other books: There are plenty of books in Category 7, above.
The one I have read over and over is Karel Capek's *The Gardener's Year* (Madison, Wisconsin: University of Wisconsin Press,
1984) which gently pokes fun at rock gardeners. And everything
written by Gertrude Jekyll is worth reading (see *The Gardener's
Essential Gertrude Jekyll* (Boston: Godine 1986).

Mail-Order Nurseries

Nurseries come and go with great rapidity. Collect as many catalogs and lists as you can until you find the nurseries that sell the plants you want. The lists often contain valuable descriptive and cultural information and can lead you into realms of gardening you had no intention of entering. The best nurseries perform the very valuable service of getting plants into cultivation, and they deserve our support. If their prices seem high, remember that even though you can raise a few plants from seed at what appears to be zero cost, the nurseries have to include in their price: time (your pleasure is their business); skill (they can usually produce a better plant than you can); and rare plant material (you may be giving away *Viola pedata* in great chunks to your friends, but *most* gardeners don't have it). And for people who garden far away from other gardeners, mail-order nurseries are the only source of clonal material.

The following is a list of nurseries I have dealt with. All are currently excellent (1987), have plants for rock gardens and wildflower gardens, and will ship. Look for others in the journals.

Colorado Alpines, P.O. Box 2708, Avon, Colorado 81620
Daystar, Route 2, Box 250, Litchfield, Maine 04350
Eco Gardens, P.O. Box 1227, Decatur, Georgia 30031
Fjellgarden, P.O. Box 1111, Lakeside, Arizona 85929
Lamb's Nurseries, E.101 Sharp Avenue, Spokane, Washington 99202
J.D. Lyon, 143 Alewife Brook Parkway, Cambridge, Massachusetts 02140
Nature's Garden, Rt. 1, Box 488, Beaverton, Oregon 97007
Pleasure Iris Gardens, 425 East Luna, Chaparral, New Mexico 88021 (Species iris)
Potterton and Martin, The Cottage Nursery, Moortown Road, Nettleton, Caistor, Lincolnshire LN7 6HX, UK. (Another good bulb source. An import license for garden-plant materials, where needed, is not hard to get.)
Rice Creek Gardens, 1315 66th Avenue Northeast, Minneapolis, Minnesota 55432
Rocknoll Nursery, 9210 U.S. 50, Hillsboro, Ohio 45133

Russell Graham, 4030 Eagle Crest Road Northwest, Salem, Oregon 97304

Siskiyou Rare Plant Nursery, 2825 Cummings Road, Medford, Oregon 97501

WeDu Nursery, Route 5, Box 724, Marion, North Carolina 28752

There are many commercial seed houses. The following are quite specialized.

Jim and Jenny Archibald, Sherborne, Dorset, DT9 5LD, England. They collect rare seed each season from a different part of the world.

Mesa Gardens, P.O. Box 72, Belen, New Mexico 87002. This is seed of succulents; many are *Aizoaceae* from South Africa and cactus seed collected in the West by Steven and Linda Brack. Some of Mesa's plants are hardy in the north.

Southwestern Native Seeds, Box 50503, Tucson, Arizona 85703. Sally Walker collects seed from the southern Rocky Mountains and the Great Basin.

There are other fine nurseries, such as Wayside Gardens and White Flower Farm. Their emphasis is on border plants. A list of such nurseries would run to pages. Avoid buying plants collected in the wild; many plants have been collected to near extinction by people who don't care about tomorrow. Creeping "civilization" is in fact a worse threat to plant life than collecting, but that doesn't excuse decimation of local populations by collectors.

Index

EPIGAEA REPENS

THE OPINIONATED GARDENER

was set on the Linotron 202 in Bembo, a design based on the
types used by Venetian scholar-publisher Aldus Manutius in the
printing of *De Aetna*, written by Pietro Bembo and published
in 1495. The original characters were cut in 1490 by Francesco
Griffo who, at Aldus's request, later cut the first italic types.
Originally adapted by the English Monotype Company, Bembo
is now widely available and highly regarded. It remains one of
the most elegant, readable, and widely used of all book faces.
The display type is Diotima italic, designed by Gudrun Zapf.

Composed by PennSet, Inc., Bloomsburg, Pennsylvania.
Printed and bound by Arcata/Halliday,
West Hanover, Massachusetts.